D0534880

GREAT COMPOSERS

MOZART

GREAT COMPOSERS

MOZART

IAN McLEAN

HAMLYN

First published in 1990 by
The Hamlyn Publishing Group Limited
a division of the Octopus Publishing Group
Michelin House, 81 Fulham Road, London SW3 6RB
and distributed for them by
Octopus Distribution Services Limited
Rushden, Northamptonshire NN10 9RZ

© 1990 The Hamlyn Publishing Group Limited

ISBN 0 600 56402 9

Produced by Mandarin Offset

Printed in Hong Kong

CONTENTS

CHILDHOOD

Although not unhappy, Mozart's childhood was far from ordinary for Leopold totally dominated his son and exploited Wolfgang's extraordinary musical talents to the full.

In the mid-eighteenth century, composers and musicians were considered little better than servants, and they were required by their masters to produce compositions for celebrations or visiting dignitaries on demand. The public concert barely existed at that time and musical performances were largely confined to the courts, the church and the noble houses. Even if a composer or musician was lucky enough to find permanent musical employment, the financial reward was generally so small he had to seek freelance commissions in order to survive. Often the only way to succeed was to find a rich patron or benefactor who was happy to provide finance in return for musical glory and high esteem.

The eighteenth century was the golden age of cultural extravagance – an era of glittering court society. Versailles, the palace of the Sun God and principal residence of the kings of France, is one of the most famous reminders of the debauchery and intrigue of this bygone age. Although Italy continued to maintain her musical supremacy, the Imperial capital of Vienna was an important culture centre, while the tiny court at Mannheim housed one of the most brilliant orchestras of the period. Many of the four-movement symphonies which were written here were to have a strong influence

on the young Mozart. It was a time, too, for the bourgeoisie and rich noble houses to flaunt their great wealth and the considerable power they wielded. Patronage of the arts was one way of achieving this aim, and without it many of the musical masterpieces would never have been performed. Much of the music written at the time was for small groups of players, often totalling no more than a dozen (the symphony orchestra began to emerge in its present form only at the beginning of the nineteenth century).

The church was also an important source of employment, and many composers, including such figures as J.S. Bach, spent their entire life in ecclesiastical service. Bach was Cantor at St Thomas' Church in Leipzig for the last twenty-seven years of his life, and most of his compositions were ecclesiastical, i.e. antiphons, masses and cantatas. Some composers, although in religious employ, were also commissioned to compose secular works.

In musical terms, the eighteenth century was a time of great change. The Baroque period, which had lasted for about a hundred years, was ending when J.S. Bach died in 1750, and new forms and expressions were emerging. The birth in 1756 of Wolfgang Amadeus Mozart, the world's most gifted child prodigy, was also the beginning of the Classical period. In a musical context,

Opposite *A 1763 painting by Carmontelle of the Mozarts in Paris. Nannerl, Wolfgang's sister, is accompanied by father Leopold on the violin and her brother on the spinet.*

the term 'classical' denotes an orderly form, devoid of any excess emotionalism and generally applies to compositions written before about 1820. This was followed by the Romantic period which began with composers such as Chopin and Schumann and lasted until the twentieth century.

THE FAMILY BACKGROUND

Leopold Mozart, the father of Wolfgang Amadeus Mozart, was born in 1719 at Augsburg in Bavaria. In 1737 he moved to Salzburg and after leaving the university where he studied theology, logic and law, he entered the service of Count Johann of Thurn and Taxis as a valet-cum-musician. Leopold was the first member of the Mozart family to be interested in music; his father was a master bookbinder in Augsburg, and other close relatives were architects or builders.

When the position of fourth violinist became vacant in the household of Archbishop Sigismund von Schrattenbach, Prince-bishop of Salzburg, in 1743, Leopold applied. He was lucky enough to be appointed and this was the beginning of his life-long musical career, although he was later to sacrifice his own musical ambitions and devote all his energies to promoting the career of his son, Wolfgang. Leopold's combination of teaching and compositional

skills clearly enhanced his musical reputation for he had a thorough knowledge of the subject. In the musical world today Leopold Mozart is considered only a minor composer, yet during his lifetime, and for some years afterwards, he was highly regarded as a teacher. In 1756, the year of Wolfgang's birth, he published a treatise entitled 'Essay on the Fundamentals of Violin Playing', or *Violinschule*. This became a standard work and earned him considerable recognition throughout Europe.

In 1747 Leopold married Anna Maria Pertl, whose father held administrative and judicial appointments at Hüllenstein and Salzburg. They were said to be an attractive couple, and although Anna was not nearly as intelligent as Leopold, she was exceedingly

Portrait of Archbishop Sigismund von Schrattenbach, Prince-Bishop of Salzburg (1698–1771), by Franz Xavier König. His relaxed rule enabled Leopold to take extended leaves of absence from his court duties in order to expoit the young Wolfgang's talents abroad.

A general view of Salzburg in 1795 with the fortress in the background; after a painting by Franz von Naumann. Salzburg has featured on the musical map of Europe since the middle of the 18th century.

good-natured and full of gaiety. Almost the perfect partner, in fact, for an austere man such as Leopold, who was noted for his stern disciplinarian outlook, and who later proved to be shrewd and calculating in the exploitation of his two children.

After their marriage, Leopold and Anna Mozart moved into the third-floor lodgings owned by a grocer, Lorenz Hagenauer, at No. 9 Getreidegasse in the old part of Salzburg, overlooking a square with a fountain. This was to be their home for twenty-five years. The house is now a museum containing all kinds of memorabilia, including Wolfgang's piano, musical scores, an array of trinkets and even a lock of his hair.

The Mozarts' marriage appears to have been a happy and united one, although at times they suffered considerable hardship and personal tragedy. Money was always a problem, particularly in the later years when Leopold barely managed to eke out an existence. Unfortunately, payment for musical scores or concerts was often in 'kind' rather than hard cash.

In the eighteenth century, poor and unhygienic living conditions meant that infant mortality was very high. Only two of the Mozarts' seven children lived beyond infancy. Their first child to survive was a daughter, born in 1751. This was Maria Anna, know in the family as 'Nannerl', who, inheriting some of Leopold's musical talents, proved to be something of an infant prodigy, although not nearly as talented as her younger brother would turn out to be.

Joannes Chrysostomus Wolfgangus Theophilus, the Mozarts' seventh child, was born on 27 January 1756, and christened with that grand name the following day in Salzburg cathedral. On that bleak, cold day, it seemed that Leopold resolved that his son would be a musician, and expressed his determination to do all he could to help achieve that end. Both Leopold and Anna fretted over their new son, fearful that he would not survive, for Wolfgang was a small, frail baby.

Leopold began to teach his children music as soon as they could walk and talk;

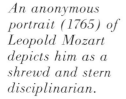

An anonymous portrait (1765) of Leopold Mozart depicts him as a shrewd and stern disciplinarian.

Above *Mozart's birthplace: the third floor of No. 9 Getreidegasse in the old part of Salzburg. The house has been turned into a museum known as the Mozarteum and contains a fascinating collection of memorabilia.*

Left *Anna Maria Mozart, Wolfgang's mother. This portrait, painted at the same time as the one of her husband seen opposite, shows a kindly, good natured woman who was much loved by her family.*

11

Wolfgang at the age of four. His father started giving him music lessons on the harpsichord even though the tiny boy had to be perched on a pile of cushions and books in order to reach the keys.

and it was while giving music lessons to Nannerl that Leopold became aware of Wolfgang's musical interest, and noticed how he reacted to sounds, musical or otherwise. Popular accounts record how the tiny boy was often to be found sitting underneath the harpsichord totally entranced by the musical sounds. Wolfgang was only four years old when he too, started to receive music lessons from his father. Within the same year he was trying to compose musical pieces of his own at the keyboard.

Leopold was so excited by the musical response shown by his small son that he enthused about them to his friend, Andreas Schachtner, the court trumpeter who also played the violin. To Leopold's dismay, Schachtner appeared unimpressed and was far more interested in discussing the adverse comments arising from Leopold's statement on the standard of music in the court.

At this period the music style in Salzburg and throughout Europe was dominated by the Italians. In court circles, where intrigue and power struggles were rife, direct questions were almost never asked in public, and answers to specially petitioned requests, if they ever came, were passed down the channels of the hierarchical structure and finally conveyed as favours. Leopold, who always thought he was better than the Italians, found it hard to conceal his feel-

ings, particularly if he saw an opportunity to further his own position. It was about this time that Leopold was hoping to take over the position of Kapellmeister, for Eberlin, the incumbent, had been ailing for a while.

As Leopold was still keen to impress his friend Schachtner with the musical skills of his son, he arranged for the court trumpeter to visit his home in order that he could hear the boy play. He hoped too, that such a visit might improve his chances of becoming Kapellmeister.

On the appointed day, the whole of the Mozart family were dressed in their best finery. For the first time Wolfgang wore knee-breeches with stockings and buckled shoes and had his hair curled in the fashionable style. The extravagant result, although the fashionable court style of the day, was exaggerated even more by the boy's diminutive size. The small boy's obvious musical ability impressed even the sceptical Schachtner, and this recognition of his talents resulted in Wolfgang's first public performance at Salzburg University. Diplomatically, Leopold included a duet by Eberlin in his son's repertoire.

When Eberlin died in 1762, however, Leopold was overlooked, and the Prince-bishop appointed Guiseppe Francesco Rolli, an Italian, to the position of Kapellmeister. This act was to sour Leopold for the rest of his life and invoke in him a deep mistrust of other musicians – Italians in particular. However, appointed to the position of Vice-Kapellmeister, Leopold found he had greater freedom and as a result he was able to devote the greater part of his life to teaching and guiding the development of his son Wolfgang and his subsequent musical career.

INTIMATIONS OF GENIUS

In spite of his frailty and propensity for illness, Wolfgang's childhood appears to have been a happy one, and although music dominated he also excelled at other subjects such as languages, particularly Italian, and arithmetic. In fact on one occasion while on tour with his father in Rome he added a postscript to one of Leopold's letters, asking Nannerl to find the arithmetic tables she had written, and to send them to him since he had totally forgotten them. It is also recorded that Wolfgang quite often made numeric calculations in the margins of his musical scores. It would appear that neither Nannerl nor Wolfgang received any formal education with other children, and both relied totally on their father for their lessons.

When Leopold realised the enormous potential of his son's musical talents, he drew up a rigid and systematic musical plan, which was strictly adhered to, day after day. Fortunately, Wolfgang had inherited his father's single-minded and obsessive qualities where music was concerned, and he studied incessantly. Whenever Wolfgang's temporary ill health forced a pause in the proceedings, Leopold waited fretfully, anxious only to resume the lessons. In fact, Leopold's dominance was such that for the next twenty years Wolfgang was hardly ever out of his father's sight. It is difficult to know just how deeply Wolfgang's mother felt about such paternal dominance and the tightly disciplined musical existence of her son: perhaps she agreed with her husband or simply found the situation easier to accept than to fight. Certainly Nannerl often resented all the attention her younger brother received.

Wolfgang was six years old when his father decided that he must show the world his children's talents, and in particular young Wolfgang's prowess at the keyboard. The decision to subject his family to such a rigorous lifestyle must have been shrewdly calculated by Leopold, for the dangers and discomforts of eighteenth-century travel were considerable. Indeed, it is almost a miracle that the Mozart family survived as well as they did, with little adverse effect other than the occasional illness. Mozart was to spend most of his short life travelling around Europe; firstly as a child prodigy, and later in search of a key musical post which he hoped would lead to some kind of financial security. In the end, this eluded him. At the beginning of 1762, the Mozart family spent three weeks in Munich, where the children played for Maximilian Joseph III, the Elector of Bavaria.

Schloss Nymphenburg, Munich, residence of Maximilian Joseph III, the Elector of Bavaria. It was here that Leopold Mozart paraded the musical talents of his children early in 1762.

FIRST RECITALS IN VIENNA

In September 1762 the Mozarts left Salzburg with a mass of luggage, including a portable harpsichord, bound for Vienna, via Passau and Linz. The reason for travelling so far north to Passau was Leopold's valuable introductory letter from Count Arco – the man who was subsequently to kick Wolfgang unceremoniously out of court – to Count Thun-Hohenstein. The Count, if he felt so disposed, could provide the introductions the Mozarts needed in Vienna, and as far as Leopold was concerned, Passau was a vital part of the plan. Vienna was renowned for its culture and vied with London and Paris as one of the musical capitals of the world. It was here at Schönbrunn palace that Emperor Franz I and Empress Maria Theresa resided.

In spite of Leopold's introductory letter to Count Thun-Hohenstein, however, court protocol could not be waived, and the Mozarts waited for three days before being admitted to the Count's presence. Not surprisingly, the Count was eager to see

Vienna was already one of the musical capitals of Europe when the Mozart family arrived in late 1762. Leopold firmly believed his child prodigy of a son would make his fortune here.

Wolfgang perform, never pausing for a moment to consider the possibility of a small boy's discomfiture at the strange surroundings, concerned only that beautiful music would be delivered on demand. Wolfgang was depressed at the sight of the fat, overbearing Count; although only six years old, he detested playing for anyone, no matter how important, if he did not think they cared anything for music. It was a trait he shared with Leopold. Yet, in order to please his anxious father, whom he considered second only to God, Wolfgang played as well as he possibly could, and Leopold received one gulden for his trouble plus the letter of introduction he so badly needed in Vienna.

The dark, cramped inn accommodation in Vienna meant that the children were unable to play the harpsichord, and when an invitation finally came from Count Collalto for the children to perform, Leopold became over-anxious in case they had forgotten all his teaching. Word had spread that the young Mozart children played with the same expertise as adults, and the nobility, with their penchant for sneering, were curious to see whether this was true. Although Leopold knew that his children possessed such adult skills, he also knew that any hint of failure in the elegant and sophisticated world of Vienna would put an end to all his plans. Leopold need not have worried – the children performed well and that single performance opened a number of important doors. A few days later the royal invitation arrived from Maria Theresa at Schönbrunn.

For the occasion, Wolfgang was dressed like a miniature courtier, complete with powdered wig and a jewelled sword – even without his musical abilities and his reputation Wolfgang would have attracted attention, and he became something of an *objet extraordinaire*. When the Imperial family first saw the Mozart children they did not think the stories they had heard regarding their musical ability could be true. Fortunately, not fully realising the importance of

The young Wolfgang is presented to Emperor Joseph II and his mother, the Empress Maria Theresa, during the Mozart family's first visit to Vienna in 1762.

the occasion, and undaunted by their opulent surroundings, both Nannerl and Wolfgang played well. It is also said that, as a test, Wolfgang played the clavier with the keys covered by the Emperor's lace handkerchief.

Some days later Leopold received a hundred ducats, court clothes for the children and an invitation to Schönbrunn the following day to play for the Empress's children.

Leopold was flattered by the gifts but Anna Maria was more sceptical, seeing the clothes for what they were – royal cast-offs! However, cast-offs or not, both Nannerl and Wolfgang wore the regal dress for the paintings that now adorn the walls of the Mozart museum in Salzburg.

It was after the second performance at Schönbrunn that Wolfgang slipped and fell on the polished floor of the palace. The small

girl who took pity on him and helped him to his feet while her royal sister went regally ahead was none other than Marie-Antoinette, the future Queen of France.

Over the next three months both children played for many of the aristocratic families, giving several performances a day and travelling from one noble house to another. Then, inevitably, Wolfgang became ill. As his condition worsened, his parents were terrified he had smallpox, and to add to the pressure Leopold received a letter from Salzburg, reminding him that his leave of absence from his court duties had long expired. Finally, scarlet fever was diagnosed, and Wolfgang began to improve. He recovered sufficiently to undertake what

was to prove a long, cold journey to Pressburg (Bratislava) on the Hungarian border to accept an invitation from some Hungarian nobles before returning to Vienna.

The Mozarts arrived home in Salzburg in January 1763. A few weeks later Wolfgang gave a violin and harpsichord performance at court, and advance notices of the occasion declared that he would play in the adult manner, improvise in a variety of styles, play with keyboard covered and identify any note that was played. The interest aroused by such publicity served only to spur Leopold on and aim for even higher goals, particularly as he had just discovered that Wolfgang could play the violin with almost as

This painting of Wolfgang, attributed to Pietro Antonio Lorenzoni, hangs in the Mozarteum in Salzburg. It shows the small boy in the formal court costume given to him by the Empress Maria Theresa.

Wolfgang's sister, eleven-year-old Nannerl, also received a set of court clothes from the royal family on the same occasion. This painting is also believed to be by Lorenzoni.

much aptitude as he showed for the harpsichord and clavier. The Mozarts remained at home in Salzburg for only six months before setting out on what was to be their first major tour, which would last until November 1766.

THE FIRST GRAND TOUR, 1763–66

T his time, in order to provide his family with at least some protection against the rigours of travel, Leopold hired his own coach. On leaving Salzburg,

the family travelled to Paris via Munich and Leopold's home town of Augsburg, where they gave several public concerts and visited relatives; Stuttgart; Ludwigsburg; Schwetzingen, the summer palace of Carl Theodor, the Elector Palatine; Heidelberg; Mainz; and Frankfurt, where Wolfgang was heard by the young Goethe and his father. This was then followed by Coblenz, Cologne and Brussels.

Leopold was able to procure introductions to most of the influential houses in all the places they visited. Word had spread of the extraordinary musical talents of Mozart, the boy genius, and Wolfgang was considered to be a star attraction. Although the children played duets as part of their repertoire, there was very little real interest in Nannerl alone. Money was the prime object of all the performances, but in spite of the children's obvious success and the incredible number of performances they gave, the family experienced mixed fortunes. It was the custom for many of the wealthy households to give in 'kind' rather than money, although all too often this payment was not received until some time after the actual performance. The profusion of trinkets and other worthless gifts is perhaps best illustrated in the letter Leopold wrote to Hagenauer, his friend and landlord in Salzburg: 'Princess Amalia, sister of Frederick the Great of Prussia, is all kisses – if only the kisses she gave my children, and to Wolfgang in particular, were louis d'or we should be fortunate; but neither innkeeper nor postmaster are paid in kisses'.

They arrived in Paris in November and it was here that Leopold hoped to make a fortune. Although they remained there for the next five months, the Mozarts found it difficult at first to break into Parisian society. And it was due only to the kind auspices of Melchior Grimm, a compatriot, that they received an invitation to spend Christmas at Versailles with a court appearance on New Year's Day. The eight-year-old

Wolfgang played the organ in front of Louis XV and the entire court.

As before, the royal patronage magically opened the right doors, this time to the French nobility, which resulted in concerts all over the capital. It was during their stay in Paris that Wolfgang's compositions appeared in print for the first time: Four Sonatas for Clavier with Violin Accompaniment, K.6–9. (The 'K' refers to the Köchel

Versailles – the palace of the Sun King, Louis XV. It was here, before the entire court, that the seven-year-old Wolfgang gave a performance on New Year's Day in 1764.

catalogue – *see* Chapter 5.) After two very successful public concerts, the Mozart family left Paris for London on 10 April 1764.

The musical scene in London must have been to the Mozarts' liking for they stayed for fifteen months, mainly at 20 Frith Street, Soho (the house has now been demolished). Wolfgang wrote his first two symphonies, K.16 and K.19, while staying for a short time at Ebury Street. Both Wolfgang and Nannerl performed a number of times before King George III and Queen Charlotte during their stay, although it is recorded that Leopold was disappointed by the fee of twenty-four guineas for each performance. But, whatever his feelings about the fee, it was greatly to the Mozarts' advantage that the sum was paid immediately.

During their stay, and as a direct result of the rather extravagant claims regarding Wolfgang's ability, the eight-year-old boy was subjected to a number of musical tests, and a report on his prowess was compiled for the Royal Society.

It was in London that Wolfgang met Johann Christian Bach, the youngest son of J.S. Bach. J.C. Bach had moved to London from Italy in 1762, and was highly regarded as a composer. Bach was to have a considerable influence on Wolfgang's music, although there is no evidence to back up the theory that he ever gave the small boy music lessons.

By July 1765 Leopold felt that they had perhaps exhausted their welcome, and at the invitation of the Ambassador to the Netherlands they left for The Hague where, despite a summons home from the Archbishop of Salzburg, they were to stay for seven months. Not long after their arrival came the news that Maria Theresa's husband, the Emperor Francis I, had died suddenly. Then Nannerl became very ill and almost died. No sooner had she begun to recover than it was Wolfgang's turn to be ill, this time with quinsy. However, both he and Leopold were well enough to play the harpsichord and violin at the celebrations

Right *A portrait of George III of England by the American painter Mather Brown. During the Mozart family's 15-month stay in London, Wolfgang and Nannerl gave a number of performances for the king and his consort, Queen Charlotte.*

Left
*Gainsborough's
portrait of Johann
Christian Bach
(youngest son of
J.S. Bach), who
settled in London
in 1762. It is
believed that he
had considerable
musical influence
over Wolfgang.*

Below *The Thames
from Somerset
House, looking
upriver towards
Westminster.
Painting by
Canaletto.*

for the coming of age of William V, Prince of Orange.

The journey back to Salzburg this time was via Brussels, Paris, Geneva – where Leopold had an introduction to Voltaire, although the audience that was promised was finally cancelled because of illness – Zurich and Munich, and they arrived home on the last day of November.

Although the strains of travelling and performing had obviously taken their toll of the Mozart family (all of them had been taken ill at some time or other), the Grand Tour was, from many aspects, an absolute triumph. It is difficult not to be amazed by Leopold's resourcefulness and ability in transporting such a young family, however talented, around Europe and arranging so many performances, both private and public. It would appear that even Anna Maria's concerns and regrets as a mother were never really voiced and certainly never affected the overall plans. It says much for Leopold's strength and that of the children that they could survive as well as they did in spite of being subjected to so much pressure, whether this was in the form of glittering adulation or just curiosity.

Not long after their return home, the archbishop asked Wolfgang to compose the music for the first act of an oratorio, *The Obligation of the First Commandment.* Michael Haydn, the court's musical director, and Anton Adlgasser, chamber composer, composed the second and third acts. It was once thought that this was a 'test piece', Wolfgang's compositional abilities still being doubted by many, who believed that Leopold composed music on his son's behalf. Modern scholarship, however, has ruled this out; the 'test-piece', composed behind locked doors at the archbishop's palace, is now believed to have been a piece of sacred music written at about the same time. At all events, the composition was well received. Even Count Karl Arco, the court chamberlain who adjudicated, was impressed when it was completed in two weeks (though Haydn commented that it was not an original composition, but in the style of Eberlin).

Some nine months later, the Mozarts were off on their travels once more. Their first destination was Vienna, and since the Mozart children were now renowned throughout Europe, Leopold expected an even greater triumph than before.

This time, however, fate played the master card and both children were struck down by smallpox. On this occasion it was Wolfgang who came very close to death. The

whole of Vienna was gripped with the pox, and for the Hapsburgs there had been another royal tragedy: the death of the Archduchess Maria Josepha. Even if the children had been well, no-one would have invited them to play in their homes, for in those days the risk of infection was deemed far too great.

When Wolfgang recovered he wrote the comic opera *La finta semplice* (K.51), but

View of modern-day Salzburg, with the Hohensalzburg fortress perched on the Mönchsberg.

because of a certain amount of court intrigue, this was never performed in Vienna. Leopold was angered by the situation but was powerless; he had made too many enemies in the court. The only recompense was a private performance of the *Singspiel* (comic opera) *Bastien und Bastienne* (K.50) at the house of Doctor Anton Mesmer. Happily this was a great success. It was the first performance of an opera by Mozart, and although full of musical clichés of the period, it is nonetheless an astonishing work for a child of twelve years. At this time, Wolfgang was also composing symphonies, divertimenti, and church and chamber music – all juvenilia and hardly ever performed today. In January 1769 the family travelled back to Salzburg, and nine months later Wolfgang was appointed to the court as honorary Konzertmeister.

Domenico Oliviero's Interno del
Teatro Regio *shows a performance of
a typical* opera seria, *with its
elaborate stage costumes, mechanical
devices and allegorical plots.*

FROM
YOUTH
TO
MANHOOD

Wolfgang's musical itinerary reads more like a travelogue – one grand tour after another followed by restless wanderings around Europe in search of fame and fortune.

It was largely owing to the Archbishop of Salzburg's benevolence that Leopold was able to set off at the end of 1769 on what was to be the second Grand Tour. This time there was no incessant wrangling regarding Leopold's leave of absence, with permission always being considered but not granted. Instead he was to leave Salzburg with the archbishop's blessing and one hundred and twenty ducats. However, the money was enough to finance only Leopold and Wolfgang and it was decided that both mother and daughter would stay at home. Although Anna Maria was dismayed at the prospect of being parted from her son, she was also filled with considerable relief at the thought of not having to set out on yet another long, arduous journey.

Leopold, although he still resented and disliked the Italian musicians, recognised the importance of Italy as a European centre

Left *The thirteen-year-old Wolfgang in Verona during his first Italian tour. This painting is attributed to Saverio dalla Rosa.*

of culture and music. It was over a century and a half since the birth of opera in Italy, and Italian *opera seria* and *opera buffa* (comic opera) had long since dominated Europe. Now it was time for Wolfgang to experience this phenomenon in its native land. In Leopold's eyes, Italy was waiting to be conquered by his son, and it was important that they undertook the Italian tour before Wolfgang became too old and began to lack some of his childish appeal. As Wolfgang was now approaching his fourteenth birthday, the trip could not be delayed any longer.

THE FIRST ITALIAN TOURS, 1769–71

The father and son's itinerary reads rather like a travelogue: Innsbruck, Rovereto, Verona, Mantua, Cremona, Milan, Parma, Bologna and Florence. However, the inclement weather at the start of their journey made even the stalwart Leopold wonder whether he had made the right decision, or whether in furthering his ambitions for the boy he had not exposed them both to unnecessary dangers. Then, as their journey took them farther south, the weather improved and with it their spirits.

It was agreed between father and son that Wolfgang would play at most of the towns where they stayed, either privately or publicly. One notable performance was at the Accademia Filarmonica, the famous music school in Mantua. He was the first person under twenty-one ever to have played there and to commemorate both the importance and the honour of the occasion, his portrait was painted in oils. At Parma they stayed at the home of the soprano, Lucrezia Aguiari, whose nickname was 'La Bastardella'.

When they arrived in Florence, Leopold and Wolfgang renewed their acquaintance with the castrato, Manzuoli, whom they had last seen in London. They also met the young English violinist, Thomas Linley, who was studying under Pietro Nardini. Linley was about the same age as Wolfgang, and the two quickly became great friends. 'Tommasino and the little Mozart, the two boy geniuses', became the talk of Italy. On his return to England Linley 'was active on a number of compositions' and might well have realised the musical world's expectations had he not tragically drowned at the age of twenty-two in a boating accident.

It was during this visit to Italy that

Opera seria *reached its peak in the late 18th century. The rigid pattern of recitative and arias never really appealed to Mozart, although he continued to write in this form until 1791, as in* La clemenza di Tito. *However, most of his* opera seria *was specially commissioned and so provided Mozart with the income he so desperately needed.*

Left *Florence, the artistic capital of Italy, with its skyline dominated by the Duomo. It was here in 1769 that Wolfgang met the young English violinist Thomas Linley.*

Below *Pope Clement XIV, who conferred on the young Wolfgang the papal knighthood of the Golden Spur.*

Above *Interior of the Sistine Chapel in the Vatican, where the Mozarts heard a performance of Allegri's* Miserere.

Wolfgang met Piccinni, Gluck's great operatic rival, for the first time.

Their arrival in Rome coincided with Holy Week and it was here that Wolfgang performed one of his most celebrated feats. On a visit to the Sistine Chapel they listened to a performance of Allegri's *Miserere*. The copyright of this nine-part choral work was jealously guarded by the papal choir and was one of the major musical preserves of Rome. Yet, on returning to his lodgings, and after a single hearing, Wolfgang wrote out the entire work from memory.

They travelled as far south as Naples, visiting Vesuvius and Pompeii, before heading north again. On their return to Rome they had an audience with Pope Clement

Hieronymus Colloredo, Prince-Archbishop of Salzburg, from an oil painting by Franz Xavier König, 1772. The kindly Archbishop Schrattenbach died in December 1771. He was succeeded by Colloredo, who was unpopular throughout his court and regarded as a tyrant by the Mozart family.

XIV, and Wolfgang was honoured with a Knighthood of the Golden Spur. From Rome they travelled to Milan, where Wolfgang composed the tragic opera *Mitridate, rè di Ponto* (K.87). The first performance was given under Wolfgang's direction a few weeks before his fifteenth birthday. The fact that a non-Italian, and a mere boy into the bargain, should compose such a triumph, is little short of a miracle.

By the end of March 1771 they were back home in Salzburg, only to leave for their second tour of Italy just five months later. This time there was a commission to write some music for the wedding festivities of Archduke Ferdinand and Princess Maria of Modena, due to take place in Milan in

October. Wolfgang's contribution, the serenata *Ascanio in Alba* (K.111), was a great success, as was a symphony in F (K.112) and a divertimento in E (K.113), which he wrote during his stay.

In December 1771 an event occurred which was to have a profound effect on both Leopold and Wolfgang's lives. The kind and easy-going Archbishop of Salzburg, Count Sigismund von Schrattenbach, died suddenly and was succeeded in the following March by Count Hieronymus von Colloredo, a wealthy member of the Austrian nobility who had given loyal service to the state and to the church. He was the antithesis of the previous archbishop, who had been rather remiss in enforcing his rule and had allowed Leopold Mozart to treat his post as something of a sinecure, with long absences abroad on the tours he undertook with his family.

The Mozarts, as well as the residents of Salzburg, were to find that the new archbishop expected servility and orderly discipline. (As time passed Colloredo became increasingly impatient with Leopold's prolonged absences, until finally, in 1777, he forbade Leopold to take any further leave for travel. The relationship between the two continued to deteriorate and in 1781, Leopold was dismissed from Colloredo's service.) At the beginning of his reign, however, Colloredo had grand ideas for the musical supremacy of Salzburg, and in his efforts to realise his ambitions, Colloredo was very aware of the considerable talents of the Mozart family and the substantial benefits those talents could bring to Salzburg. In August 1772 Colloredo appointed Wolfgang leader of the court orchestra, and later the same year he gave the Mozarts permission to leave on what was to be their third and last tour of Italy. Wolfgang's most important compositions during the summer preceding their departure to Italy were seven symphonies (K.124, K.128–30, K.132–4); four divertimenti (K.131 and K.136–8); and six string quartets (K.155–60) – a truly prodigious output.

THE THIRD ITALIAN TOUR, 1772–73

During their third tour of Italy they stayed mainly in Milan. Wolfgang had scored such a huge success here with his opera *Mitridate* on his first tour in 1770 that he was commissioned to write a further *opera seria*, *Lucio Silla*, K.135. When Wolfgang arrived in Milan on 10 November, he had written very little of the opera, but because he was able to work very quickly, he completed the entire score in six weeks – in time for the first performance on 26 December. Despite initial difficulties, mainly with the singers, *Lucio Silla* was well received, and was performed twenty-six times.

During his visit, Wolfgang composed what was to become one of his most celebrated vocal works, the solo cantata, *Exsultate jubilate*, K.165. From Leopold Mozart's point of view, the main purpose of the tour was to secure a musical appointment for Wolfgang, either in Milan or in

Florence, at the court of the Archduke Leopold of Tuscany. However, such an appointment was not forthcoming, and since they had already overstayed their allotted time, both father and son returned to Salzburg in March 1773.

Shortly after their return, the Mozart family moved to a spacious new home with eight rooms, overlooking what is now known as the Makartplatz. Leopold felt that they now needed more space, for Nannerl was twenty-two and Wolfgang was seventeen years old. He did not tell his family of his decision until all the arrangements had been made, so the proposed move came as a shock to Anna Maria and the children.

The month of July found the Mozarts in Vienna again. Leopold was still searching for a musical position for Wolfgang and hoped to secure a position for him at the court of

Empress Maria Theresa. Although Leopold and Wolfgang had an audience with the Empress at Schönbrunn, Leopold's hopes of a key musical position for his son were dashed once more, and in October they returned to Salzburg. But while in Vienna, Mozart composed several works in a form that had first occupied him seriously in Milan – the string quartet. After he returned to Salzburg he directed his creative energies elsewhere, and it was only when he was living in Vienna in the 1780s that he produced his masterworks in this genre. Another musical form he was to excel in, and which he first attempted in late 1773, was the string quintet. His first composition was in B Flat, K.174. The string quintet was first established as a musical form by Michael Haydn, brother of the famous Joseph. He had added an extra viola part to the conventional string quartet in order to obtain a richer, fuller harmony.

During the latter part of 1773 and the beginning of 1774 Wolfgang composed several symphonies, divertimenti and serenades. If these youthful compositions had been written by any other composer in the mid-eighteenth century, they would have been highly regarded, particularly today; but because Wolfgang went on to create such masterpieces, the early pieces are considered to be exercises in craftsmanship.

Then Wolfgang was commissioned to write an opera by the Elector of Bavaria, Maximilian Joseph, for the Carnival festivities in Munich at the end of 1774. The new *opera buffa*, *La finta giardiniera* (K.196), was written in the Italian style of the day, and the Elector requested Wolfgang's presence at the first performance. Surprisingly,

Milan was the scene of many of Wolfgang's early successes. It was here that the operas Mitridate *and* Lucio Silla *and the celebrated solo cantata* Exsultate jubilate *were first performed in public.*

and largely because he didn't want to offend his powerful neighbour, Archbishop Colloredo gave Wolfgang permission to travel to Munich. Once again Leopold saw this as an opportunity to further Wolfgang's career with a court appointment but once more it was to lead to frustration and bitter disappointment.

INTERLUDE: WORK AND PLAY

This portrait of the 21-year-old Wolfgang, dated 1777, shows him wearing the Order of the Golden Spur.

For the Mozarts, the next two years were fairly quiet and uneventful. During 1775 Wolfgang wrote his five violin concertos, K.207, K.211, K.216, K.218 and K.219. All the concertos are scored for oboes, horns and strings only. Although none of these concertos is as important as the piano concertos, they

contain many of the Mozart traits to come rather than the formal clichés of the day, although Wolfgang was not slow to exploit the fashionable trends of the period. One example is the way in which he suddenly breaks into a 'Turkish' theme at the end of the third movement of K.219. This style of music was immensely popular in Vienna and indeed the whole of Austria at that time.

Wolfgang composed a great deal of church music during 1776–7 for the various ecclesistical events that took place in the Cathedral. The most important of the secular works were the *Serenata Notturna* (K.239) for double orchestra, the concerto for three pianos (K.242), two divertimenti (K.247 and K.251), and the serenade in D major (K.250). Most of this music was specially commissioned by the wealthy families of Salzburg. The concerto for three pianos was written for the Countess Lodron and her two daughters, both of whom were

Wolfgang's pupils. The serenade was commissioned by Sigmund Haffner, a former Bürgermeister of Salzburg, to celebrate the marriage of his daughter.

In January 1777, Wolfgang produced the piano concerto in E flat (K.271), which was commissioned by the French virtuoso, Mlle Jeunehomme. This was the first of Mozart's great concertos for this instrument and the first to carry the unmistakable stamp of the greatness to come. The highly original andantino was in the form of an operatic recitative, with the piano imitating what would have been the vocal part.

At the archbishop's request Wolfgang composed *Il rè pastore* for a state visit by Archduke Maximilian Franz. Although the Archduke was pleased by the performance, Wolfgang did not receive any payment. This lack of feeling and musical appreciation from Colloredo and the rest of the court made Wolfgang resent the restrictions of provincial Salzburg even more.

It was at this period in his life that Wolfgang's character began to undergo a marked change, perhaps largely due to the fact that his entire childhood had been dominated by his severe and studious father. From the age of four, Wolfgang's life had been filled with music and learning, and Leopold's strict disciplinary rule had never been seriously questioned. Now all that was to change, for the new, impulsive Wolfgang was full of fun and high spirits. It seemed that his one aim was to be the life and soul of the party. He wanted to fill his life with dancing and girls, play billiards and idle away his time. Work, even if it was his beloved music, suddenly seemed less important, and what little money he earned disappeared on mere frivolities. His increasing high spirits and coarse sense of humour – some of Mozart's early biographers were amazed by the lewd jokes and obscenities

Below *A mid-18th century domestic scene by Januarius Zick showing musicians vying with the attractions of gossip over coffee and a game of billiards. To his father's horror, Wolfgang became an avid billiards player and would often spend all night at the table with his friends.*

found in his letters – inevitably affected his court compositions and, finally, his relationship with Colloredo. Leopold was shocked by the feckless activities of his son, and Wolfgang's changed outlook eventually led to a breakdown in the relationship between father and son.

As far as Archbishop Colloredo was concerned there was very little purpose or gain to the court from Wolfgang's secular compositions, and the increasing demand for the younger Mozart's work only fuelled Colloredo's dislike and resentment. He grew more and more tyrannical towards both father and son, until this finally grew into open dislike.

Leopold's continued requests to the archbishop for leave of absence were simply ignored or refused, and ultimately it was this protracted persistence by Mozart senior that led to the first dismissal of them both; Leopold, however, received a reprieve shortly afterwards.

Right *Mannheim, in spite of its relatively small size, was a leading centre of musical life in Europe in the latter half of the 18th century.*

Below *Carl Cannabich, who was a successful composer at the court of Mannheim and a great friend of the Mozarts. He introduced Wolfgang to the Weber family.*

ON TOUR AGAIN, 1777–79

Although Wolfgang was now twenty-one years old, the marked changed in his character meant that his father no longer felt able to trust him. Finally, Leopold decided that his wife, Anna Maria, should accompany Wolfgang on his next tour. It was with a heavy heart on 23 September 1777 that Leopold bade farewell to his wife and the son whose triumphs he had shared, and, until this moment, whose entire life he had moulded. Their departure was a poignant moment, and Leopold was not to know that he would never see his wife again.

The first stop on the tour was the Bavarian capital of Munich, followed by Augsburg, Leopold's birthplace. Here they were warmly received by other members of their family, and Wolfgang enjoyed some innocent flirtatous fun with his young cousin, Maria Anna Thekla. During his stay he visited Johann Stein, the piano-maker.

From Augsburg they travelled to Mannheim, one of the greatest musical centres of the eighteenth century. It was famous throughout Europe for its resident orchestra and style of playing: the controlled crescendo and diminuendo was part of the orchestral technique, written into the score by the group of composers in the service of the court. The Mannheim symphony was the forerunner of the classical symphonies

which were later composed by both Haydn and Mozart. Wolfgang was also enthused by the inclusion of flutes and clarinets within the resident orchestra.

Although no formal court position was available, Wolfgang was soon immersed in the musical life of Mannheim, giving music lessons to the children of the court musicians and composers, such as the Cannabichs, Wendlings and Danners. It was through his friendship with Christian Cannabich, the director of instrumental music, that Wolfgang met the Weber family – a meeting that was to cause his father even greater distress and which would affect the relationship between them for the rest of their lives. Fridolin Weber, a minor singer and prompter at the local theatre, had four

Left *The Wendling sisters, Elisabeth and Dorothea, became great friends of Wolfgang and his mother, whom they first met during their stay in Mannheim. The sisters were renowned singers and Wolfgang composed several arias and operatic parts for them.*

daughters and a son, and it was not long before Wolfgang had fallen deeply in love with Aloysia, the second daughter. The sixteen-year-old Aloysia was indisputably pretty and, to add to her attractions for Wolfgang, she had a lovely, although untrained, soprano voice. Wolfgang, at the instigation of the Webers, was persuaded to write to his father, suggesting that he should cancel his trip to Paris and join forces with the Weber family instead. The Webers' idea was that they could all tour Italy, the home of musical excellence, and make their fortune there.

Leopold read the letter with increasing despair. All his fears about the foolhardy behaviour of his son were beginning to come true. Nevertheless, the news from Wolfgang

came as a great shock. Instead of adopting his usual dictatorial role, Leopold wrote a pleading letter to his son, explaining how he had sacrificed his whole life for Wolfgang and how, at this moment in time, he and Nannerl were living in increasingly straitened circumstances yet were still making extraordinary savings in order that Wolfgang might take every opportunity to exercise his talents. Letter followed letter – each one imploring Wolfgang to keep to the original plan and reminding him of his filial duties and solemn vows.

So, on 14 March 1778, Wolfgang and his mother climbed into the carriage and set out for Paris, a journey that was to take nine days. In spite of the hostilities between Prussia and Austria over Bavaria, the inherent dangers of travel were far from the Mozarts' thoughts. For her part, Anna Maria Mozart experienced an enormous sense of relief that her son had at last bowed to his father's wishes, while Wolfgang, having been persuaded to part from the desirable Aloysia, suffered the entire journey with a very heavy heart.

During the sojourn in Mannheim, Wolfgang produced several compositions, including concert arias for Aloysia Weber, Anton Raaff and Dorothea Wendling; six violin sonatas (K.301–6), two flute concertos (K.313–4), and two flute quartets (K.285 and K.298) – the commissions for the last were arranged by Dorothea Wendling's husband for the Dutch flautist, De Jean.

Wolfgang was not particularly fond of the flute – nor, for that matter, of De Jean, perhaps because the fee for the commission was never paid. The resultant concertos are not considered to be among Mozart's best compositions. However, nothing that Wolfgang wrote is negligible; these compositions are certainly among the best ever written for the flute, and they still feature regularly in the concert repertoire.

The stay in Paris was not a success, for the city of 1778 was certainly not the one which the Mozart family had visited in 1764. The two musical factions in the operatic circles of Paris – the followers of Piccinni and those of Gluck, were engaged in the battle between the old, tightly-knit regime and the new,

enlightened regime personified by the philosopher Rousseau. Wolfgang cared little for the talents of Piccinni, and even less for the views of Rousseau. What did they know about music? In turn, it seemed that Paris cared little for Mozart. Wolfgang's amazing childhood talents had long been forgotten and his small, unprepossessing figure as a young man gave little indication of his musical genius. No doors were magically opened and Wolfgang found life increasingly difficult. Again it was Melchior Grimm who came to the rescue, this time with an introduction to the Duke de Guines, a powerful man in the French court and a friend of Marie-Antoinette. The Duke, who had studied under the celebrated Rameau,

played the flute surprisingly well. De Guines' daughter played the harp 'agreeably well' and the doting father asked Wolfgang if he would instruct her in composition. Wolfgang willingly agreed, but in a letter to his father he complained that she was totally lacking in any original ideas. However, grateful for the Duke's generosity, Wolfgang wrote the concerto for flute and harp (K.299) for them. Unfortunately, he was further disenchanted when the Duke left Paris for the country without paying Wolfgang for any of the lessons.

At this time Paris was one of the few cities in Europe to hold public concerts. These were known as the Concerts Spirituels, and the Director, Jean Le Gros, asked Wolfgang

An 18th-century chamber concert in the salon of a great house. The audience seems to be devoting its attention less to the music than to the observation of social niceties. (Engraving after a painting by Augustus de St Aubin.)

to write the *Sinfonia Concertante* (K.ANH9/297B), and a symphony, the 'Paris' (K.297). The sinfonia concertante was a hybrid work, rather more a symphony than a concerto, with obligato solo parts. The concertante parts were written for three of the famous Mannheim orchestra's wood-wind players and the virtuoso horn player and composer Giovanni Punto. Predictably, given the pervasive atmosphere of intrigue and envy in the city's musical world, the score disappeared before it could be per-formed. (It was almost a century later before a copy of the score was discovered, when the flute part was found to be scored for oboe and the horn part was written in a higher register. Even to this day, no-one is sure if this is a genuine Mozart composition or a skilled rewrite of the original by a lesser composer. Because of the doubt relating to this work, the Köchel catalogue refers to it as K.ANH9.)

In May Wolfgang was offered the position of organist at Versailles, but the salary was so pitiful he could not afford to accept. Then Noverre, the ballet master at the Académie Royale de Musique, asked Wolfgang to write the music for his ballet, *Les petits reins*. Enthused, Wolfgang quickly set to work, hoping that, if the work pleased, a commis-sion for an opera might follow. The ballet was given its first performance on 12 June – but Wolfgang's name was omitted from the programme and Noverre received all the

J.N. della Croce's group portrait of Nannerl, Wolfgang and Leopold, painted c. 1780, is now in the Mozarteum at Salzburg. A framed portrait of Wolfgang's mother, who had died in 1778, is in the background.

credit. The music was found in the Académie's archives in 1872, although the first six numbers of the score were not by Mozart and he had termed them 'miserable old French airs'.

The first performance of the 'Paris' symphony was on 18 June and this was a resounding success: it made full use of the sixty players in the orchestra, including the large and rich-sounding wind band with clarinets, the very first time Wolfgang had ever included these in a symphony. (Mozart influenced Haydn in this respect.)

On 3 July, shortly after the first performance, his mother, who had been ill for some weeks, died. Although Wolfgang had written to his father and sister telling them how

ill Anna Maria was, he found himself quite unable to write and tell them of her death. Instead he wrote to a family friend in Salzburg, Abbé Bullinger, and asked him to break the news to his father. Anna Maria Mozart was buried in one of the cemeteries attached to St Eustache. To Wolfgang's dismay, Melchior Grimm did not attend the funeral, and the relationship between the two men deteriorated even further when Wolfgang was unable to repay the money he owed the Baron.

In August, Wolfgang had the good fortune to meet Johann Christian Bach, his old friend from London. Wolfgang always held J.C., as he was known, in great esteem. In his youthful admiration of the older composer, Wolfgang had arranged three of 'J.C.'s' piano sonatas as concertos, and added the string parts himself.

On hearing of Bach's death in London in 1782, Wolfgang wrote: 'You will have already heard that the Englishman, Bach, is dead. What a loss to the musical world'. Since Wolfgang's Paris trip was little short of a fiasco, Leopold felt he had no other choice but to beg Colloredo to re-employ his son. Surprisingly, the archbishop agreed, and Wolfgang re-entered his service as court organist, a position which became vacant on the death of Adlgasser during Wolfgang's stay in Paris.

After his mother's death Wolfgang had become increasingly unsettled. But, much to Leopold's dismay and concern, he had not returned home directly from Paris. Aloysia was still very much in his thoughts and, wishing only to see her again, he travelled to Mannheim. On his arrival, and much to his disappointment, he found that the newly appointed Elector of Bavaria, Carl Theodor, had moved most of the court musicians, including the Weber family, to Munich. Wolfgang's stay in Mannheim was quite short, and each day he hoped that some kind of musical post would become available at the opera house. In the end he was ordered to return home by his father. Leopold was concerned that his son's prolonged absence might jeopardise the position of court organist which he had secured for him. However, Wolfgang, in the hope of seeing Aloysia, travelled instead to Munich. There, to his dismay, he discovered that Aloysia no longer returned his love. Her fortunes had changed – she was now a rising star, earning a considerable salary, and was no longer interested in a penniless composer. In fact she was to marry an actor, Josef Lange, before Wolfgang met her again in Vienna in 1781.

Stuart Burrows as Idomeneo, King of Crete, in a production of Mozart's early opera seria.

THE
MIDDLE
PERIOD

*The coming of musical maturity in the adolescent Mozart saw the
final break from Archbishop Colloredo, his patron in Salzburg, and
Wolfgang's subsequent move to Vienna.*

Wolfgang finally returned to Salzburg in January 1779, a somewhat chastened young man. His mother had died, he had lost the woman he loved, and he had failed to find either a rich patron to sponsor him or any musical appointment. He had little option but to bow to his father's wishes and return to the service of the Archbishop of Salzburg. Above all he needed to earn some money in order to help repay some of the family's debts.

The following two years were not very happy. Even though Wolfgang was at home and under his father's watchful eye, Leopold no longer felt able to trust his son. Wolfgang, eager to become independent, felt increasingly stifled by the restrictive social conventions of provincial Salzburg. One reason for his discontent was the lack of a resident theatre company, for opera had become one of Wolfgang's great passions. Salzburg, unlike Munich and Mannheim, had to rely on visiting touring companies. To add to his discontent, Wolfgang's freedom was curbed by his obligation, as court organist at the cathedral, to carry out any duties requested of him.

Left *Interior of
the cathedral at
Salzburg.
Wolfgang was
appointed court
organist to the
cathedral in 1779,
and many
ecclesiastical works
of his middle
period were first
performed here.*

A PERIOD OF CONSOLIDATION

Over the next two years, however, he was to write two of his more important church works. First came the Mass in C (K.317), known as the 'Coronation', in March 1779, followed by *Vesperae solennes de confessore* (K.339). The Mass was probably written for the 'Crowning of the miraculous image of the Virgin', at the church in Plain, a place of pilgrimage at that time, just north of Salzburg. This festive Mass is for four soloists and orchestra, including trumpets and drums. In the Agnus Dei of both this mass and its succesor, K.337, there are striking anticipations of the two great arias, 'Dove sono' and 'Porqi amor', sung by the Countess in *The Marriage of Figaro*. It says much for Wolfgang's skills that he was able to compose a liturgical work for the restricted requirements of Archbishop Colloredo and yet, at the same time, imbue it with such symphonic and operatic technique. Then early in the following year, Wolfgang com-

pleted two settings of the Vespers, although the one most often performed today is *Vesperae solennes de confessore*. Both these settings are the glory of Mozart's Salzburg church music, and the Laudate Dominum for soprano solo from the second set (K.339) is one of music's supreme examples of quiet rapture.

In the orchestral and instrumental field it was a time for development and consolidation: the most profound and impressive work is the *Sinfonia Concertante* in E flat (K.364) for violin, viola and orchestra. This is Wolfgang's second hybrid work – it is not a concerto but a symphonically constructed work with important parts for a variety of solo instruments, written in the style developed by the Mannheim school of composers. In it he reaches new heights of richness in melodic invention with a marvellous interplay between the violin and viola soloists. The slow movement has an unforgettable serenity and spiritual beauty.

In a much more joyful mood is the concerto for two pianos (K.365) which Wolfgang composed for himself and Nannerl. A sparkling work, full of fun and

Emanuel Schikaneder, the theatrical impresario and actor who Mozart first met in Salzburg in 1780 when he was asked to write the incidental music for the play, Thamos, König in Aegypten.

Emperor Joseph II, by Anton von Maron. On the death of his mother, Empress Maria Theresa, in 1780, Joseph became emperor in his own right. He did much to encourage the evolution of a specifically German opera in preference to the Italian style which dominated the musical scene at this time.

humour, its interweaving of the piano parts provides attractive tunes and is technically brilliant.

The two symphonies, K.318–9, written in 1779, and symphony K.338, written in 1780, are typically Salzburgian. They are scored for strings, oboes, bassoons and horns – all are good workaday Mozart symphonies and the last to appear before the series of masterpieces in this genre.

For pure entertainment there are the two serenades, K.320 and K.361, and the divertimento, K.334. The first minuet from K.334

has been one of Mozart's most popular works ever since it was first composed. In 1780 Emanuel Schikaneder visited Salzburg with his theatrical touring company and Wolfgang was asked to provide additional incidental music for the production of *Thamos, König in Aegypten*, a play written by Tobias von Gebler, whom Wolfgang had first met in Vienna in 1773, when he wrote the music for two of the choruses.

In November 1780 the Empress Maria Theresa died and her son, Joseph II, who had co-reigned with his mother for fifteen

George Frederick Handel. Mozart admired Handel and re-orchestrated two of his best-known works, the masque Acis and Galatea *and the oratorio* The Messiah, *for performances at Vienna in the winter of 1788.*

An elaborate theatrical performance was held to celebrate the marriage of Joseph II and Isabella of Parma. This painting by Meytens hints at the glamour of the occasion.

years, finally became Emperor in his own right. Now, with total power, Joseph brought sweeping reforms and a new relaxed period of rule.

IDOMENEO

I t was about this time that Wolfgang received a commission from the Elector of Bavaria, Carl Theodor. The Elector required a grand *opera seria* composed in the Italian tradition for the next Munich carnival. *Idomeneo* was Wolfgang's first opera of enduring quality. The libretto was commissioned from Gianbattista Varesco, the court chaplain in Salzburg. Since Wolfgang knew the librettist and some of the singers, he was able to compose at an even greater speed than usual, and in November he set out for Munich.

Left *The heroine Constanza in a performance of* Die Entführung aus dem Serail, *which was first performed in 1782.*

Opera seria was a traditional form which dated back to the time of Handel in the eighteenth century, and consisted of a rigid pattern of successive recitatives and arias. It was an essential part of court entertainment until 1780, and was performed on state occasions such as weddings or coronations.

The two female lead singers were the Wendling sisters, Dorothea and Liesl; Anton Raaff, whom Wolfgang had already composed for, was one of the male leads. Vincenzo Dal Prato, the leading male soprano, was unknown and particularly difficult, perhaps because he had never performed on stage before. In the end, Wolfgang was reduced to teaching him his part, note by note. Notwithstanding all the crises attached to the production of an opera, the delayed first performance eventually took place on 29 January 1781, two days

Christoph Gluck, one of the most influential opera composers of his day, whom Mozart succeeded as Imperial court composer in 1787.

A view of the city hall of Munich in the mid-18th century. The capital of Bavaria, Munich was one of Mozart's favourite cities – though he was never able to secure a musical appointment there.

after Wolfgang celebrated his twenty-fifth birthday.

Both Leopold and Nannerl journeyed from Salzburg for the first performance. Unfortunately, very little was recorded about this momentous occasion, perhaps because the family were all together and there was no need for the customary exchange of letters. *Idomeneo* was an indisputable success. Much of the opera is in the Gluckian tradition but Wolfgang's remarkable creative powers established *Idomeneo* as one of the most important examples of *opera seria*.

Opera seria was not, however, a musical form which Wolfgang really enjoyed, and the only other example he was to write was *La clemenza di Tito*, for the coronation of Emperor Leopold II as King of Bohemia, in Prague in September 1791.

THE BREAK WITH THE ARCHBISHOP

As usual, the Mozarts overstayed their leave – there were many attractions in Munich, and since Archbishop Colloredo was visiting Vienna there seemed little need for a hasty return. Enjoying their new-found freedom, Leopold and his family even journeyed to Augsburg to visit their relatives. However, their absence from Salzburg and the neglect of their court duties did not pass unnoticed. Wolfgang was summoned by the archbishop to join him in Vienna. He set out immediately, reaching Vienna on 15 March.

What happened next has tended to become distorted, with Archbishop Colloredo cast as the villain of the piece, and Wolfgang

in the role of the poor, down-trodden genius. There is no question but that Colloredo was a stern disciplinarian who enjoyed the power that his exalted position gave him. Although he recognised Wolfgang's unquestionable genius, and the musical advantages and prestige he brought to his court and to Salzburg's cultural position in Europe, he nevertheless looked upon the young man as someone who had, for far too long, been allowed to follow his own musical desires and who, in so doing, had shirked many of his musical obligations and responsibilities at court. In Colloredo's eyes, Wolfgang was a minor official – a court organist, and as such, a servant, albeit a rebellious one.

Like his father in his youth, Wolfgang resented the whole idea of servility; court procedure, rules and regulations were highly restrictive and impinged on his creative genius. Now, fresh from his musical triumph and freedom in Munich, Wolfgang suddenly found himself answerable once more for his every move to the archbishop and the more exalted members of his entourage. He was obliged to have his meals with the other servants, and Wolfgang commented bitterly to his father that at least he was placed 'above the cooks' at the dining table. Wolfgang went out of his way to flout the archbishop's orders. He thought that, as so many of his friends in Vienna belonged to the nobility and had also declared their dislike for Colloredo, he could count on their support. He was wrong: no ruling house could support open rebellion by a mere commoner, no matter how great a genius he might be.

The final break came in May 1781 when, during a particularly angry audience with the archbishop, Wolfgang was unceremoniously dismissed from the service of the court and supposedly kicked from the room by the chief steward, Count Arco.

Utterly humiliated, Wolfgang wrote a tirade of abuse about Archibishop Colloredo to his father at home in Salzburg. At the same time he reassured his father and told him not to worry, as he, Wolfgang, saw a rosy future for himself in Vienna. Not unnaturally, Leopold was horrified at his son's outburst and the shame of Wolfgang's dismissal from the service of the archbishop. In desperation, Leopold tried to smooth things over with the court in order to have his son reinstated. This time, however, Wolfgang was determined to go his own way and he ignored all his father's advice and remonstrations. Leopold continued in the archbishop's service, but the breakdown in

Joseph Lange's portrait of Constanze, the painter's sister-in-law. Constanze and Wolfgang were married in 1782, much against Leopold's will.

relations between father and son was such that Wolfgang returned to Salzburg only once more during his lifetime.

In June 1781 Wolfgang moved into lodgings with his old friends, the Webers. Fridolin had died in 1779, and his widow had moved to Vienna with her unmarried daughters, Josepha, Sophie and Constanze. Wolfgang spent a great deal of his time with the family and it is not surprising that after a considerable amount of scheming by the mother to push the two together, Wolfgang found himself falling in love again and finally becoming engaged to Constanze. At this time Constanze was eighteen years old, and a promising singer, although no great beauty.

When Leopold discovered his son's whereabouts he was almost beside himself with worry. Unable to contain his concern and anger, he wrote to Wolfgang ordering him to leave the house at once. This Wolfgang did in July.

During the summer months, most of the nobility and the wealthier families moved to the country, and Wolfgang found that without the distractions of any pupils he had considerably more time to himself; time which he could devote to composing. He composed three sonatas for violin and piano (K.376, K.377 and K.380) and a wind serenade in E flat (K.375) for two clarinets, two bassoons and two horns; and at this time he also began work on the opera *Die*

50

Entführung aus dem Serail (The Abduction from the Seraglio, K.384). The latter was written because Emperor Joseph II wanted to encourage a true German style of opera rather than the foreign, mainly Italian style that flourished in Vienna at this time. After such a directive, it is rather strange that the subject for the opera was not a German-style *Singspiel* but a Turkish divertimento, all about ladies being saved from an oriental harem by their lovers. However, in the late eighteenth century, anything with an oriental flavour was very fashionable, and many composers, including Wolfgang, attempted to satisfy popular demand.

Although Wolfgang composed the opera in great haste, as was his style, it was not until the middle of 1782 that *Die Entführung* was staged. As usual, a succession of intrigues and petty jealousies, far worse than those experienced with *Idomeneo*, caused the inevitable postponements. However, all the work and heartache was worthwhile, and from the very first performance the opera was an enormous success. As a result, *Die Entführung* was Wolfgang's most often performed work during his lifetime. It was this composition that revealed the composer's remarkable gift for operatic comedy. There are the highly amusing moments when Osmin, the amorous but buffoon

figure of a Turkish servant, is finally outwitted by the lovers, and moments of heartfelt sadness that musically are sheer joy. It has often been called the first German opera; certainly it was one of the roots from which all later German opera was to spring.

During this time, Wolfgang continued to give lessons to several pupils, including Josepha Palffy (who perhaps surprisingly was a relative of Archbishop Colloredo) and Josepha Auernhammer. The latter was the daughter of a Viennese councillor and so ugly that Wolfgang poked merciless fun at her. As a result of this lighthearted relationship, Josepha fell hopelessly in love with Wolfgang, although this was not reciprocated. However, he was so impressed by her playing he revised his concerto for two pianos in E flat (K.365), which he had written during the summer of 1776, for her. To this he now added clarinets, trumpets and drums. This was followed by the heavenly sonata for two pianos in D (K.448).

MARRIAGE

I n December 1781 Wolfgang was trapped by Frau Weber into signing a marriage contract, and he wrote to his father telling him of his desire to marry Constanze. The reaction from the father who

A scene from the Royal Opera's 1987 production of Die Entführung aus dem Serail.

had dominated Wolfgang's life from the moment he had been born was, not surprisingly, one of total opposition. Leopold wrote back to his son, withholding his consent.

It was around this time that Wolfgang also produced the first two major works of a long succession of masterpieces; these were two serenades, the first of which was an orchestral piece commissioned by the Haffner family in Salzburg for the ennoblement of their son Sigismund. The serenade was sent to Salzburg, but soon afterwards Wolfgang asked for the score to be returned. By the beginning of 1783, and after considerable reshaping, the work was relaunched as his symphony in D major (K.385), now known as 'The Haffner'. The second serenade was for wind octet in C minor (K.338); this great work also exists as a string quintet (K.406).

By August Wolfgang could no longer hold out against the scheming Weber family and on the fourth of that month he and Constanze were married in St Stephen's cathedral, the day before Leopold's consent was finally received. The wedding breakfast was given by Baroness Waldstätten.

Unfortunately, Constanze was weak in both health and character and unable to provide the kind of support that Wolfgang, now free of the disciplined and orderly existence imposed so rigidly by Leopold, needed. During their marriage, Wolfgang and Constanze moved from one set of lodgings to another, as their finances dictated. Money was frittered away the moment it was received, and if Wolfgang was unable to earn enough to support his sometimes flamboyant lifestyle, he borrowed heavily from friends. In the later years of his life, begging letters were despatched to all and sundry, seemingly with little compunction on Wolfgang's part. Constanze contributed little to their domestic orderliness. In the ensuing nine years she was to bear her husband six children, although only two survived infancy, and the numerous pregnancies added to her general lassitude. (Wolfgang himself had never enjoyed robust health and the ceaseless demands made by Leopold on him as a child, the endless wandering, and now an unstable lifestyle would all eventually contribute to his early death at the age of thirty-five.)

Mozart's marriage contract, dated 3 August 1782. After many months of scheming by Frau Weber and the threat of legal action, Wolfgang and Constanze were finally married on 4 August 1782.

Although Wolfgang and Constanze's fortunes varied somewhat, they did not starve, and they soon adapted to the pattern of married life. Wolfgang's day generally began by giving lessons to the children of the minor nobility and the wealthier families living in Vienna. He usually travelled to his pupils' houses and when the lessons were over Wolfgang often stayed to lunch or accepted other invitations from friends. Lunch was invariably followed by a game of billiards, a pastime much to his liking. Music, however, was never far from his thoughts, and there are many contemporary records of Wolfgang pausing in the middle of a game of billiards to jot down a theme that occurred to him. It is also widely reported that he tapped incessantly on anything that came to hand – a habit, however musical, that must have been irritating to his companions. It appears that composition was not always quite as easy for Wolfgang as the Mozart myth would have us believe. Although Wolfgang was an un-doubted genius and could create pieces in his head before setting them down on the page, he often preferred to write his ideas down and then re-work them in much the same way as any other composer.

COMPOSITIONS AND CONCERTS

By the end of 1782, Wolfgang had started a series of compositions that included the six string quartets he subsequently dedicated to his friend, Joseph Haydn; these compositions were written over a period of a little over two years, and the last was not composed until the beginning of 1785. Wolfgang had met Haydn the previous year, and immediately the two men became firm friends, with no hint of any professional jealousy that had marred so many of Wolfgang's other relationships with composers in Vienna.

The other compositions in the series were two horn concertos (K.417 and K.447) and three piano concertos (K.413–5). The horn concertos were probably written for Joseph Leutgeb, a horn player in the Salzburg court orchestra before he moved to Vienna. The

St Stephen's cathedral, Vienna, where Wolfgang and Constanze were married.

Das Konzert, *a mid-18th-century engraving by Charles Eiser. At this time concerts were intimate affairs. It was only in the late 1790s that they began to evolve into the large-scale form familiar to modern concertgoers.*

manuscripts of the horn concertos abound with Wolfgang's ideas of practical jokes: K.417 has the comment that he has taken pity on the ass, ox and fool (Leutgeb); and a later horn concerto of 1786 (K.495), is written in different coloured inks.

The concertos were of course written for the instruments of the period – in this case a valveless horn – and Wolfgang showed an astonishing grasp of the characteristic capabilities of this rather limited instrument without making any concessions to the soloist in either the cantabile slow movements or the jolly hunting rondo-type finales.

Apart from the money he earned giving music lessons, Wolfgang's main source of income at this time was from subscription concerts. These concerts were usually held in the grand houses of Vienna, in much the same way as we would give a formal dinner party today. However, depending on the social position or wealth of the host, such concerts were sometimes open to the public. At these concerts, Wolfgang would play a piano concerto and hope for a small financial

profit as well as the subsequent subscription of either the full or a reduced score. All too often he was disappointed, as happened with the three concertos (K.413–5). The subscribed publication was a flop, and as Wolfgang had taken out a loan to finance the cost of publication and the creditors were demanding payment, he was forced to turn to his friend, Baroness Waldstätten, to help him out of his difficulties.

This kind of situation was to repeat itself over and over again for the next nine years until his death. He almost invariably organised his subscription performances carelessly and was far too sanguine in his expectations of the financial returns. And whenever the inevitable crises ensued, he was much more inclined to rely on the generosity of his friends than to help himself. In such matters, in short, he conformed to the stereotype of the feckless, unworldly genius.

By far the most important concert that Wolfgang had arranged to date took place on 23 March 1782. Emperor Joseph II attended and heard, among other compositions, the

'Haffner' symphony and the new piano concerto in C major (K.415). Unfortunately, as had happened so often before, the royal presence brought great acclaim but scant financial reward.

In the late autumn of 1782, Constanze became pregnant, and the journey they had planned to Salzburg was postponed until the following summer. Their first child, a boy, christened Raimund Leopold, was born on 17 June. Unhappily, the infant lived for only two months, and died on 19 August while his parents were in Salzburg.

Before their departure for Salzburg, Wolfgang was very concerned that the Archbishop Colloredo, knowing that he was visiting the city, might have him arrested on some trumped up charge. Leopold did his best to allay Wolfgang's fears in the many letters that passed between them before the visit.

Wolfgang had written a new Mass in C minor, K.427, or at least he had finished some of the movements, before his marriage to Constanze. He took this with him to Salzburg, and completed it for the first performance in St Peter's Church, with Constanze singing the part for solo soprano. Apart from the motet *Ave verum corpus* (K.618) and the uncompleted *Requiem* (K.626), the C minor Mass, or what survives of it, was Wolfgang's only liturgical work after leaving the archbishop's service in Salzburg.

During Mozart's lifetime, music-making often took the form of an impromptu gathering of friends, and even formal concerts mostly took place in private houses.

At this time the court concertmaster was Michael Haydn, brother of the celebrated Joseph and an old friend of the Mozarts. Haydn was not enjoying very good health and was finding it difficult to complete a commission for the archbishop. Wolfgang went to this friend's aid and composed two duos, K.423–4, for him, although at the time – and certainly in the archbishop's eyes – these compositions came from the pen of Michael Haydn and not from that of his ex-organist. If only Colloredo had known!

Wolfgang and Constanze's visit to Salzburg was not a success. Although both Leopold and Nannerl were polite to Constanze, there was little warmth in their welcome and the strained atmosphere must have come as a disappointment to Wolfgang. There were no open disagreements during their stay, but it must have been with some relief that the couple ended their visit and left for Vienna in late October.

Wolfgang and Constanze travelled via Linz, where they were invited to stay with the now very elderly Count Thun. The Count asked Wolfgang if he would write a new symphony for a concert to be given on 4 November. The request was made on 31 October – allowing four days for the composition! Completely undaunted by the proposition, Wolfgang sat down and composed the 'Linz' symphony (K.425) in the required time. It is a wonderfully festive work, employing trumpets and drums but lacking in flutes and clarinets (possibly these latter instruments were not available in the Count's household). The clarinet was a fairly recent addition to the orchestra in 1738, and there were relatively few musicians who could actually play the instrument at that time.

Wolfgang and his wife returned to Vienna in December to discover that their infant son had died in August. Infant mortality was still commonplace, and although the news was possibly not unexpected, it still came as a shock.

A large part of 1784 was dominated by domestic issues rather than major musical output, for although Wolfgang was composing for much of the time he produced few master works. During the summer he was ill for several weeks with what would now be diagnosed as acute kidney trouble. On a happier note, and much to Leopold's enormous relief, Nannerl married Baron von

The beginning of a violin sonata composed by Mozart in 1782. In the top right-hand corner is Wolfgang's dedication, in French, to 'my dear Wife'.

Berchthold zu Sonnenburg, on 23 August. The couple went to live in St Gilgen, a small town just outside Salzburg, where her mother had lived as a child. The Baron was fifteen years older than Nannerl and had five children from a previous marriage. Nannerl bore him three children, a son and two daughters, although only the son survived. On the death of the Baron in 1801, Nannerl and her son returned to live in Salzburg. Constanze became pregnant for the second time, and another boy, Carl Thomas, was born on 21 September. This child was to live until 1858.

WITH HAYDN IN VIENNA

It was during 1784 that Wolfgang showed an increasing interest in freemasonry. Freemasonry was not considered anti-religious at this time, in spite of a certain amount of tension with the Catholic church, and in December Wolfgang was admitted to the Beneficence Lodge. Haydn was also a mason for a short time but joined the lodge where the scientist, Ignaz von Born, was the master. Many other leading figures were also freemasons, and the principle of universal brotherhood was a great attraction to Wolfgang, who was also deeply religious. His membership must also have given him a certain degree of security, for in the last years of his life, Wolfgang was to become more and more dependent on his freemason friends for financial support.

One member of the brotherhood who became a friend of Wolfgang's was the clarinettist, Anton Stadler. This friendship, coupled with Stadler's virtuoso capabilities, is responsible for the wealth of compositions for clarinet in the Mozart repertoire – all of these were dedicated to Stadler.

It was at this time that Haydn, who usually resided at the country estate of Prince Nikolaus Esterházy, was staying at his patron's residence in Vienna, where Wolfgang was invited to play. Their earlier friendship was renewed, and Wolfgang completed the six string quartets he dedicated to Haydn. The string quartet is possibly one of the most difficult musical forms, yet Wolfgang was not quite thirty-six years old when

Count Thun surrounded by the symbols of freemasonry (engraving after a painting by Rahmel, 1787). Mozart was greatly attracted to the freemasonry movement and was admitted to the Beneficence Lodge in 1784. Many of his later compositions have hidden masonic connotations.

Right *Schloss Esterházy at Eisenstadt, the country estate of Prince Nikolaus, the rich and generous patron of Joseph Haydn. Mozart was invited to play at the prince's Vienna residence in 1784.*

Below *A Vienna skyline, dominated by St Stephen's.*

he wrote these brilliant compositions. By comparison, Haydn was nearly fifty years old when he composed his masterpieces.

Early in 1785, Leopold made the long, cold journey from Salzburg to visit Wolfgang and Constanze in Vienna. During Leopold's stay, Wolfgang invited von Dittersdorf, Vanhal and Haydn to his home for a musical evening, where they played Wolfgang's string quartets. Leopold was stunned by the beauty of the performance,

and even more impressed when Haydn said to him: 'Before God, and as an honest man, I must tell you that your son is the greatest composer I know.' That comment from Haydn, one of the greatest and most respected composers of the time, must have been hugely gratifying to Leopold.

Shortly after meeting Haydn, Leopold was further rewarded for all his sacrifices when he watched his son perform in the presence of the Emperor Joseph II. The

Joseph Haydn (seen here in 1792, when he was 60) was the brother of Mozart's friend Michael, who was also a musician and court composer to Archbishop Colloredo in Salzburg. Joseph Haydn, regarded as the greatest composer of his day, was an early teacher of Mozart and generous in acknowledgement of Wolfgang's genius.

evening was a tremendous success and, after what had been something of an emotional visit, Leopold returned to Salzburg with proud memories of his son and the fond belief that the whole of Vienna was at Wolfgang's feet.

Wolfgang's main compositions during late 1784 and 1785 were the piano concertos. All the mature masterpieces flowed from his pen during this period, which together with the following year, was the zenith of his

musical recognition and success in the capital. From that moment on, however, his fortunes were to decline rapidly.

The concertos began with the G major (K.453) and was followed by the B flat major (K.456), which was commissioned, probably during Wolfgang and Constanze's visit to Salzburg, by the blind pianist Maria Theresia von Paradies, who was on a concert tour of Europe. Then came a group of three (K.449–51), the F major (K.459), and the dark D minor (K.466). This last was first performed shortly after Leopold's arrival in Vienna. It was regarded for many years as Wolfgang's most overtly Romantic concerto; indeed, Beethoven was so impressed by its quality that he composed cadenzas for the two outer movements. The slow movement is headed *Romanze*, a most unusual title for a concerto movement.

The piano concerto in C major (K.467) which followed employs horns, trumpets and drums, and a light, festive mood prevails once more. (The limpid beauty of the andante, coupled with today's cinema screen connotations, have made this the most widely performed Mozart concerto of the past decade.)

AN ENGLISH CONNECTION

Wolfgang continued to give music lessons in order to earn money. There was a small English community living in Vienna at this time, some of whom became Wolfgang's pupils. He would

Title page of the first edition of the six quartets Mozart dedicated to Joseph Haydn. The compositions were partly inspired by Wolfgang's admiration for Haydn's work in this genre.

SEI
QUARTETTI
PER DUE VIOLINI, VIOLA, E VIOLONCELLO.
Composti e Dedicati al Signor
GIUSEPPE HAYDN
*Maestro di Cappella di S.A.
il Principe d'Esterhazy & &
Dal Suo Amico*
W.A.MOZART
Opera X.

*In Vienna presso Artaria Comp.
Mercanti ed Editori di Stampe Musica,
e Carte Geografiche.*

often play in quartets at the lodgings of Stephen Storace and his sister Nancy. Stephen was one of Wolfgang's pupils, the son of an Italian double-bass player who had settled in London but had sent his children to Italy for their musical training. Nancy sang with the Italian opera and was in Vienna to fulfil a number of engagements. The nineteen-year-old Nancy was as attractive to look at as she was to listen to, and not long after their meeting, Wolfgang wrote the part of Susanna, in *Le nozze de Figaro* (The Marriage of Figaro), for her.

Another of Wolfgang's pupils was Thomas Attwood who, after his return to London, became organist at St Paul's Cathedral. (He was later to act as host to the young Mendelssohn when the composer visited London in the early 1830s.) A third young man was Michael Kelly, who had been born in Dublin in 1762 and was a member of the same Italian touring company as Nancy Storace. He, too, sang in the first performance of *Figaro*, and he became a very close friend of Wolfgang's. Both men enjoyed a game of billiards, and Michael was to write a detailed account of their friendship some years later.

Anna Selina Storace as Euphrosyne in Comus. *Anna, known as Nancy, and her brother Stephen became close friends of Wolfgang, who greatly admired Nancy's voice and wrote several pieces for her.*

THE
LAST YEARS

After a lifetime of financial insecurity and failure to secure permanent employment in any of Europe's musical establishments, Wolfgang's health finally broke down.

The summer of 1785 was a significant point in Wolfgang's life, for this was when he first met Lorenzo Da Ponte at the home of Baron Wetzlar. Da Ponte, born Emmanuele Conegliano, was a converted Jew, who before settling down in Vienna had led a dissolute life with a reputation almost as notorious as Casanova's, despite the fact that he had taken holy orders. Although Da Ponte had worked with other opera composers, including the revered Antonio Salieri in Vienna, he had never found anything like the fame and recognition that would come from his col-

Opposite A portrait of Mozart painted in 1816 by Barbara Krafft.

Left A scene from the Royal Opera's 1987 production of Le Nozze de Figaro.

laboration with Mozart. It was Da Ponte who provided Wolfgang with the librettos for the *The Marriage of Figaro, Don Giovanni* and *Così fan tutte*.

The Marriage of Figaro was the second play in a trilogy written by the French playwright Beaumarchais. The first, *The Barber of Seville*, had already been turned into an opera by Paisiello and had become a triumphant success during the early 1780s. (Paisiello's opera was later to be replaced in the public's affections by Rossini's version of 1816.) Lorenzo Da Ponte may not have been the greatest poet in the land but he was certainly shrewd and instantly recognised Mozart's musical genius. For his part, Wolfgang also recognised the usefulness of Da Ponte.

The play on which *The Marriage of Figaro* was based had been banned by the Emperor Joseph II, following a similar ruling in France, because he thought it would cause subversion and revolution among the populace. The only chance of such an opera being staged in Vienna depended on all the revolutionary elements being excised from the libretto and on the powers of persuasion of Da Ponte himself. Luckily the Emperor relented.

The first performance was scheduled for 28 April 1786, but because of the inevitable theatrical intrigues it was postponed. A dance was arbitrarily cut out of the third act; fortunately the Emperor, who was invited to attend the rehearsal, thought the result rather strange and, when told what had happened, demanded that the missing passage be reinstated. It seems that Salieri, the court composer and an obvious rival of Wolfgang's, was largely responsible for the attempts to ruin the performance. In fact the squabbling became so intense at one point that Wolfgang threatened to throw the score in the fire. *The Marriage of Figaro* was eventually staged on 1 May. Nancy Storace played Susanna, Francesco Benucci was Figaro, the baritone Steffano Mandini sang Count Almaviva and the soprano Laschi

Lorenzo da Ponte, the librettist for three of Mozart's operatic masterpieces, Figaro, Don Giovanni *and* Così fan tutte.

Antonio Salieri, whose reputed envy and mischievous plotting against Mozart have been exaggerated over the years. He was undoubtedly a great rival of Mozart's during Wolfgang's final years, but he was a successful composer in his own right.

was the Countess. Wolfgang's close friend Michael Kelly played Basilio.

The first performance, with Wolfgang conducting from the keyboard, was such a success that on the third night the demand for encores doubled the performance time. However, the royal involvement was such that the Emperor ordered that 'no piece for more than one voice' was to be repeated. In spite of such tremendous acclaim a further six performances only were given before the fickle Viennese switched their allegiance to *The Doctor and the Apothecary* by von Dittersdorf and *Una cosa rara*, the work of a minor Spanish composer. The next performance of *Figaro* did not take place in Vienna until 1789 when Wolfgang composed two new numbers for it. In musical circles today *The Marriage of Figaro* is considered to be one of the most perfect operas ever composed.

Several other compositions occupied Wolfgang during the latter half of 1785 and the few months before the stage production of *Figaro* in 1786. The first was the masonic funeral music (K.477); a darkly scored piece, solemn yet not sombre, it was written to commemorate the deaths of two fellow masons. As in other compositions Wolfgang wrote for the lodge, there is a prominent part for the basset-horn, possibly because one of the other members was an expert player of that instrument.

The violin and piano sonata in E flat (K.481) was followed shortly afterwards by more piano concertos: the E flat (K.482), the A major (K.488) and the C minor (K.491). All these concertos show Mozart at the peak of his inspiration, and no two are similar; for example, much of the A major is brilliant and lighthearted, while the C minor is dark and dramatic.

During the winter of 1785–6 Wolfgang received a commission from the Emperor Joseph II for a short theatrical piece, to be performed in the Orangery at Schönbrunn, in honour of the Governor-General of the Netherlands. The work chosen was a dull satire on the theatre, more a play than an opera, with a great deal of spoken word, called *Der Schauspieldirektor* (The Impresario, K.486). It is rarely performed, even today, largely because of the tedious dialogue.

On 18 October 1786, Constanze Mozart gave birth to their third child. It was another boy, christened Johann Thomas Leopold, but the baby died less than a month later.

TRIUMPH IN PRAGUE

Increasing financial problems forced Wolfgang to consider another trip to England and he toyed with the idea of taking up residence there in preference to staying in Vienna, particularly if there was the chance of earning more money. However, an important part of the plan was to lodge the then two surviving children with Leopold. Not surprisingly, Wolfgang's father refused; so the English trip was postponed and the family set off for Prague in January 1787.

Most of the compositions that appeared around this time were chamber works – two piano trios (K.496 and K.502), the sublime sonata (K.497) for piano duet, the string quartet (K.499) known as the 'Hoffmeister', and the trio for clarinet, viola and piano (K.498). The last, with its unusual combina-tion of instruments, was originally written for Anton Stadler, the clarinettist, and Franziska von Jacquin, a favourite piano pupil, with Wolfgang himself playing the viola, an instrument he loved.

When Wolfgang and Constanze arrived in the Bohemian capital, Prague was in the grip of 'Figaro fever', and they were treated like royalty wherever they went. The opera was such a success that arrangements in the form of quadrilles and waltzes were being played all over the city and the 'catchy airs' were whistled in the streets.

Before Wolfgang left Vienna for his visit to Prague he had composed a new symphony which he took with him. The work, scored for a 'grand orchestra', was given its pre-mière during his stay in the Bohemian capital and is known as the 'Prague' sym-phony (K.504). It is regarded as one of Mozart's greatest symphonic achievements and is the only symphony of his maturity in three movements, dispensing with the cus-tomary minuet.

Bondini, the impresario responsible for staging *The Marriage of Figaro*, and enjoy-ing what would now be called a 'box-office

A view of Prague, its skyline dominated by Hradčany castle. Wolfgang and Constanze spent many happy hours in the Bohemian capital – away from the financial worries and heartaches of their life in Vienna.

success', gave Wolfgang another commission. The new opera was due to be produced the following season, but even more welcome was the advance of a hundred ducats. Their spirits boosted, Wolfgang and Constanze enjoyed their visit enormously, staying at the home of Count Thun. They spent a considerable amount of time in the company of the Dušeks, whom they had first met in Salzburg. Franz Dušek was a well-known piano player, composer and teacher, and his wife Josepha was a soprano of some repute. On his return to Vienna, Wolfgang contacted Da Ponte and enlisted his help for the libretto of the new opera. Perhaps because of his reputation as a libertine, and perhaps with tongue in cheek, Da Ponte suggested that Wolfgang might consider Don Juan as a subject.

The legendary Don Juan was an early seventeenth century rake who, with the help of his servant, Leporello, committed one act of villainy after another. Don Juan was finally dragged down to Hell for his sins by the ghostly statue of the Commendatore of Seville, a nobleman he had murdered. In fact Don Juan was so unrepentant, he foolishly invited the statue to dinner! However, as the last words of the libretto proclaim: 'In this life scoundrels always receive their just deserts.'

An opera, by the Italian composer Gazzaniga, based on the same theme, already existed under another title; and a ballet called *Don Juan* by Gluck had been performed in Vienna during the 1760s.

Although Wolfgang possibly set to work on the new commission immediately, it was very much his style to leave polishing of the final composition until the very last moment – often playing the music at the rehearsals and adapting it to suit the singers. According to a number of contemporary reports, he would write down the musical form shortly before the ultimate rehearsal and only just in time to have the score copied for the musicians on the opening night. In order to complete *Don Giovanni* on time, Wolfgang returned to Prague in September, and was joined by Da Ponte in October. It is said that they were lodged in houses on opposite sides of the street and kept up a considerable repartee through their open windows. During the rehearsals, Da Ponte received con-

A silhouette of Mozart in the Dušek's house in Prague. The Dušek's were generous friends of Wolfgang and Constanze and often entertained the young couple during their visits to the city.

siderable help and advice from the ageing Giacomo Casanova himself, who at that time was librarian in the household of a Bohemian nobleman and was engaged in writing his memoirs.

DEATH OF LEOPOLD

I n 1787 Wolfgang's English pupils left Vienna and, en route for England, paid a visit to Leopold in Salzburg. According to a letter from Nannerl to Wolfgang, Leopold was by this time a very sick man. He died suddenly on 28 May, but it was some days before Wolfgang received the news of his death. It appears that Wolfgang, largely preoccupied with his own misfortunes at this time, had rather distanced himself from the real world. The news of Leopold's death was not unexpected, and it did not appear to have any immediate emotional impact on Wolfgang. But in fact it must have affected him profoundly. In 1784 he had begun to compile a catalogue of his works in an attempt to keep track of his huge output. A catalogue entry for May 1787 reveals how, as a composer utterly absorbed in his work, Wolfgang nevertheless expressed the pain and sorrow of his life at this time. For there, composed just before his ailing father's death, is listed one of Mozart's most profound masterpieces, the string quintet in G minor (K.516). Some of Wolfgang's most poignant music is written in the minor key, and this work is no exception; and its slow movement, although in the major key, is one of Wolfgang's most moving compositions.

The next work Wolfgang listed in his catalogue is one of his most popular compositions. It is the serenade K.525, scored for a small string band and called *Eine kleine Nachtmusik*. It is one of his most perfect creations, and one which since its very first performance has remained a favourite with audiences throughout the world.

In October Wolfgang and Constanze returned to Prague with the unfinished manuscript of *Don Giovanni*. They stayed with their old friends the Dušeks in their house in the middle of a vineyard on the outskirts of Prague.

Once again tantrums and squabbles among the performers and the inevitable backstage intrigues threatened the first performance. The première of *Don Giovanni* was finally staged on 29 October. *Don Giovanni* is a very different opera from *The Marriage of Figaro* and Wolfgang was

The Dušek's house, 'Bertramka', in Prague. In Mozart's day the house was outside the city in the middle of a vineyard.

Mozart performing before Emperor Joseph II. Wolfgang's position of Imperial court composer, although prestigious, did not provide him with the financial security he sought.

rather uncertain about its reception with the public. He need not have worried, for it was an instant success. Following such acclaim, the Mozarts were in no hurry to leave Prague. Constanze was pregnant again but, since the baby was not due until late December, they were able to extend their stay for a few days and enjoy themselves. Not surprisingly, both were reluctant to return to the domestic cares and financial

hardships awaiting them in Vienna.

On 12 November, three days after their return to Vienna, Christoph Gluck, one of the most celebrated and influential composers of the age, died aged seventy-three. Three weeks later Emperor Joseph II appointed Wolfgang to the position of Imperial Court Composer. However, Wolfgang's hopes of financial security were short-lived. The salary was reduced to eight hundred

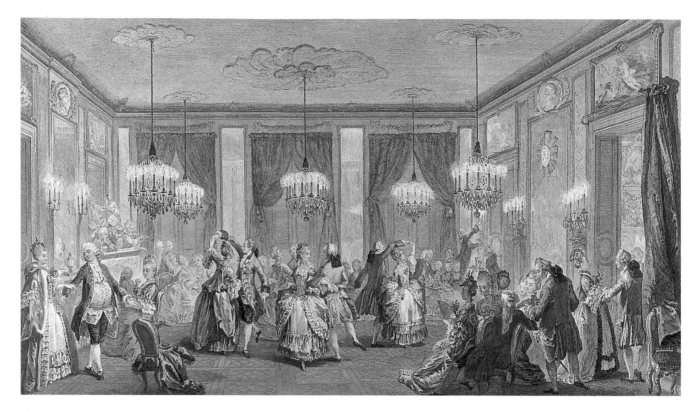

An 18th-century ball: an engraving after a painting by Augustus de St Aubin. Dancing was all the rage in Vienna at this time and Mozart, as court composer, provided countless contra-dances and minuets for the imperial balls.

Right A scene from the Glyndebourne production of Don Giovanni in 1982. Even the music from such serious works provided the basis for quadrilles performed on the dance floors of Vienna in Mozart's time.

florins, less than half the amount Gluck had recieved. Nor did the Imperial duties match Wolfgang's expectations. All the requests for musical compositions were for countless dances for the Imperial balls held at the Redoutensaal, and in particular for the carnival season. Although Wolfgang enjoyed dancing and was known to host such all-night festivities at his home, there is no doubt that such a limited repertoire would have palled. All Wolfgang's dances were written for the Redoutensaal programme and many other famous composers, such as Haydn and Beethoven, also provided music for these festive occasions. The dances were divided into two groups: minuets for the aristocracy and contra-dances for the general public.

Constanze gave birth to a daughter, Theresia, on 27 December. This child lived for only six months, dying on 29 June 1788.

The first performance of *Don Giovanni* in Vienna was held on 7 May 1788. It was not a success, owing largely to the almost inevitable bickering between several of the singers and requests for new or easier arias. In this performance Aloysia Lange, Wolfgang's sister-in-law, sang the part of Donna Anna, Francesco Albertarelli played the Don and Francesco Bussani sang the Commendatore and Masetto.

Wolfgang's position at court was not eased by the fact that he was a member of the freemasons; for suddenly, in the Emperor's eyes, the order had become the cause of all the capital's troubles. Wolfgang and many

of his friends who also belonged to the radical movement found themselves prime targets for vilification.

This volatile situation affected Wolfgang's financial position, for his freelance work, on which so much depended, became increasingly difficult to obtain. In the end Wolfgang was reduced to writing one begging letter after another. One of his friends and a recipient of many of the letters, was fellow-mason Michael Puchberg who, during the next three years, was to give Wolfgang considerable financial support.

One of music's greatest paradoxes also occurred at this time. In quick succession, Wolfgang composed three supreme masterpieces of the symphonic form. Between the months of June and August 1788 he produced the symphony in E flat major (K.543), the G minor (K.550), and the C major (K.551), better known as the 'Jupiter'. The other major composition of this period is the string trio (K.563), perhaps his most underrated and little known master-

piece. It is dedicated to Michael Puchberg, and there is much conjecture about its hidden masonic meaning.

In an attempt to save money, for they were unable to meet the pressing demands of their landlord, Wolfgang and Constanze moved to the outskirts of Vienna in June. However, living so far out soon proved to be impracticable and they were forced to return to the centre of the city. In order to supplement his income, Wolfgang re-orchestrated two of Handel's best-known works, the masque *Acis and Galatea* and the oratorio *The Messiah*, for a concert given by Baron van Swieten, a wealthy patron of the arts. (It was Swieten's translation of James Thompson's Romantic verse that was set by Haydn for his last oratorio, *The Seasons*.)

PRUSSIAN JOURNEY

In the spring of 1789 increasing financial problems forced Wolfgang to accept an invitation from Prince Carl von Lichnowsky to accompany him to Berlin. As always, Wolfgang lived in perpetual hope of obtaining a prestigious musical appointment and this time he fervently hoped that the musical King of Prussia, Frederick William II, might offer him such a position at court. Wolfgang and the Prince travelled north in Lichnowsky's private coach, via Prague, Dresden and Leipzig. They stopped to visit friends en route, and Wolfgang earned a hundred ducats in Dresden for a performance given to the Elector of Saxony, Frederick Augustus III.

Frederick the Great, King of Prussia, was a keen musician and composer in his own right. Mozart's last three string quartets were dedicated to him.

In Leipzig Wolfgang met the organist of St Thomas' Church, Johann Friedrich Doles, Bach's successor. The new cantor was seventy-four years old; he gave Wolfgang a warm welcome and invited him to play the organ that Bach had made so famous. Wolfgang gave a public performance and amazed his audience with the skill and sensitivity of his playing.

On arriving in Prussia, Wolfgang divided his time between Berlin, where a performance of *Die Entführung* was given in his honour at the National Theatre, and Potsdam, where the Prussian King's court resided. The King was a generous benefactor,

and Wolfgang received a handsome fee as well as a commission to compose six string quartets. The King was a very competent amateur cellist, and in order to pander to his host's ego, Wolfgang composed some rather elaborate and flattering solo parts. However, the quartets were not written until after Wolfgang returned home. Before travelling back to Vienna in May, Wolfgang went to Leipzig to give another concert. By chance, Josepha Dusek was also visiting the area and sang the new concert aria, 'Non temer, amato bene' (K.505), with Wolfgang playing the commanding part for piano obligato.

Constanze, who suffered from indifferent

health, became ill again during the summer months. She was expecting their fifth child and, when Wolfgang succeeded in borrowing some money, she was despatched to Baden, the fashionable spa resort, in order that she might partake of the 'cure'.

In August there was a revival of *The Marriage of Figaro*, and shortly afterwards the clarinet quintet (K.581) was performed for the first time. This is one of Mozart's finest pieces, a miraculous composition, particularly by someone beset by so many financial and domestic problems.

On 16 November, Constanze gave birth to a daughter, but the baby died the same day.

Then, just as their financial situation became particularly critical, the Emperor inadvertently came to the rescue with a commission for another opera. Once again Wolfgang turned to Da Ponte for the libretto, and once again the result was quite different from either *Don Giovanni* or *The Marriage of Figaro*. The new work was a comedy of intrigue and manners with some dark undertones called *Così fan tutte*. The first performance was held on 21 January 1790, and was a notable success with the Viennese. Unfortunately, the success was short-lived. The Emperor Joseph II died a month later and court mourning closed all

Così fan tutte was the third opera composed by Mozart with libretto by Lorenzo da Ponte.

Emperor Joseph II and (left) his brother, Grand Duke Leopold of Tuscany. (Portrait by Batoni.)

the theatres until the summer.

Two more string quartets (K.589 and K.590) were written in May and dedicated to the King of Prussia. The remainder of the commission were never written, owing mainly to Wolfgang's ill-health. Although he managed to sell the first three completed works, the fact that they had been commissioned by the King did little to increase their value.

Wolfgang hoped he would succeed Salieri as director of the opera when the latter was forced to retire because he was out of favour with the new Emperor, Leopold II. However, once more Wolfgang was to wait in vain, and the choice this time was Joseph Weigl, the Austrian composer. Both Wolfgang and Constanze suffered more ill-health during the summer months, and once again Constance travelled to Baden to take the waters. To add to Wolfgang's disquiet, there was considerable gossip concerning her amorous behaviour there. Once again fellow freemason Michael Puchberg came to

Wolfgang's aid and provided him with the much needed financial assistance.

Later in 1790 the Imperial Court moved to Frankfurt-am-Main, where Leopold II was to be crowned Holy Roman Emperor. Wolfgang was not included in the official party but he decided to go at his own expense, eager to have the opportunity of earning some money from concert-playing. He organised and played in a concert, and he was idolised by the inhabitants of Frankfurt, but none of the adulation generated the money he so badly needed.

On his way back to Vienna, Wolfgang played in Munich for the Elector of Bavaria and the visiting King of Naples. As always, he was well received in the city: how he must have wished he could remain there and escape from his domestic troubles!

During the winter he received two invitations to visit England – the first time by O'Reilly, a promoter of Italian opera, the second by the impresario Johann Salomon, who was in Vienna and about to accompany his friend Joseph Haydn on his first successful tour. Wolfgang could not accept either of the invitations: it is ironic that, as his musical reputation grew, so did his poverty.

At that time there was no protection against copyright infringement and Wolfgang received no payment for either the sale or the performance of his works. Two major compositions at this time were the string quintet in D major (K.593) and Mozart's last piano concerto, in B flat major (K.595). These were followed by workaday compositions, including minuets and contra-dances for the winter ball season, together with three trifles for mechanical organ.

THE FINAL YEAR

Then, in the spring of 1791, came a curious and unexpected request from his old friend Emanuel Schikaneder for music for a magic pantomime called *Die Zauberflöte* (The Magic Flute). Schikaneder had staged such works at the Freihaus Theatre, and since they had not been true opera the performances had attracted large, if not very discriminating, audiences. On this occasion, however, whatever Schikaneder's description, the work was an opera in its truest sense. Like Wolfgang, Schikaneder was a mason, and the opera is full of masonic symbolism; but this in no way detracts from the enjoyment of either the story or the music.

Constanze, although in poor health, was once again pregnant, and in order to revive her flagging spirits she went to stay in Baden. It was during one of Wolfgang's visits to Baden to see his wife that he composed a short ecclesiastical motet, *Ave verum corpus* (K.618), his first church music since the Mass in C minor (K.427) of 1783. On 26 July Constanze gave birth to a boy, Franz Xavier Wolfgang: happily, this child survived infancy and lived until 1844.

Above *Pietro Metastasio, a great librettist who collaborated with many 18th-century composers.*

Left La clemenza de Tito, *completed only three months before Mozart's death, was based on a libretto by Metastasio.*

July also brought the commission for the Requiem (K.626). For many years the provenance of this commission was shrouded in mystery and a certain amount of romanticism, but it would appear that it was really a very straightforward matter. A wealthy but untalented amateur musician by the name of Count Franz Walsegg wanted to pass off a requiem as his own composition. What better composer to write such a work than Mozart? The deception failed, however, for Mozart died before the work was completed and the unfinished score was found by Constanze amongst Wolfgang's papers after his death. Constanze passed the work first to Josef Eybler and then to Wolfgang's pupil, Süssmayer, for completion.

In spite of illness and a feeling of overwhelming exhaustion July was a busy month for Wolfgang. *The Magic Flute* was not quite finished and the Requiem hardly begun when he received a commission for an opera from the authorities in Prague. Rather belatedly they wished to celebrate the crowning of Leopold II as King of Bohemia.

Since it was going to be a very public occasion an *opera seria* was required. Wolfgang was asked to write the music for *La clemenza di Tito*, a Roman tragedy concerned with intrigues and the burning of the Capitol during the reign of the Emperor Titus.

In August the Mozarts, accompanied by Wolfgang's pupil Süssmayer, travelled to Prague. Wolfgang made a super-human effort to complete the opera in time for the first performance on 6 September. The finished work, although it was a good example of *opera seria*, was not well received.

Wolfgang's continuing ill-health was by now causing considerable concern amongst his friends, and he left Prague for the last time in mid-September. On his return to Vienna, Wolfgang was immediately involved in the rehearsals for *The Magic Flute*, yet he managed to find time to write the sublime clarinet concerto (K.622) for his friend Anton Stadler.

Wolfgang conducted the first few perfor-

The opening of the 'Lacrymosa' from the Requiem (K.626), a sublime work unfinished at Mozart's death.

Engraving of a stage setting for Act 1 of The Magic Flute, *first performed at Prague in 1791.*

A silverpoint drawing by Doris Stokes – the last known portrait of Mozart.

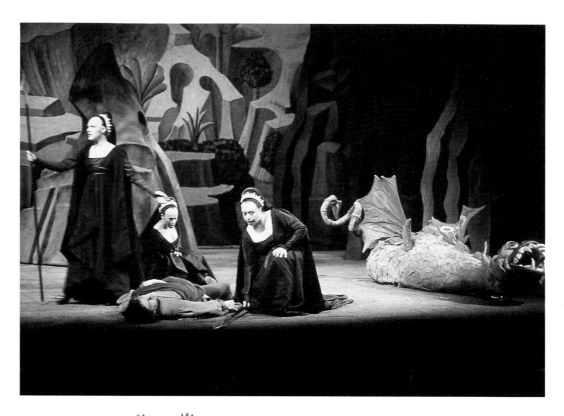

This scene from The Magic Flute *shows Tamino being saved from the monster by the attendants of the Queen of the Night.*

Right *Papageno, the birdseller with his magic pipes: a costume design from an 1819 production of the opera.*

mances of *The Magic Flute* himself, and although initially audiences were rather unappreciative, it was not long before the opera became a great success, playing to full houses night after night. Over twenty performances were given in October alone, and the enthusiastic reception must surely have boosted the composer's flagging spirits, particularly since Salieri, Mozart's great rival at that time, was often to be seen at the performances.

In spite of Wolfgang's deteriorating health, Constanze left her husband to fend for himself and returned to Baden in October. On 20 November, Wolfgang took to his bed and during the following two weeks suffered from very high fever and severe headaches. His hands and feet became swollen and he underwent severe bouts of sickness. When Constanze returned she found her husband weak and melancholy. He grew weaker each day until he no longer had the energy or the concentration to work on the Requiem. Then, early in the morning on Monday, 5 December 1791, Wolfgang died.

The custom at that time demanded almost immediate burial without any pomp or ceremony. Michael Puchberg refused any further financial assistance and Baron van Swieten paid for a third-class funeral. This took place on 7 December. The small group of mourners included Süssmayer, Albrechtsberger and, surprisingly, Salieri. Constanze was too ill to attend. There was some confusion about the arrangements, and Wolfgang was finally laid to rest in a common grave with five or six other corpses in accordance with contemporary burial custom in Vienna. There has always been considerable speculation regarding the ultimate cause of Mozart's death, and a strong rumour that Salieri poisoned him in an envious rage. The most likely cause of death, however, was rheumatic fever, a disease that Mozart had contracted as a child.

A portrait of Wolfgang and Constanze Mozart's two sons, Carl Thomas (1784–1858) and Franz Xavier Wolfgang (1791–1844) – the only two of the Mozart's six children to survive infancy.

The Mozart Memorial in Vienna. Mozart moved to Vienna after leaving Salzburg in 1781 and lived there for the rest of his short life.

Wolfgango Amadeo Mozart

THE MUSIC

*In Wolfgang's lifetime only his fellow genius Joseph Haydn and
a few others perceived the true stature of Mozart's work. Today it
is recognised as a supreme pinnacle of Western art.*

Wolfgang Amadeus Mozart's music is one of the greatest glories of European civilisation. Unlike many composers whose work is restricted to just one genre – Verdi, Wagner and Mahler, for instance – Mozart composed master works in a wide range of forms, including symphonies, concertos, quartets, masses and operas. Even as a small boy Mozart composed works that were technically brilliant, whatever musical form he chose. As he matured as a person, so did his work: the later the date, the greater the masterpiece. He was also an accomplished musician and played a number of instruments, such as the harpsichord, clavier, violin and viola. Among his musical contemporaries were such distinguished names as Gluck and Boccherini, yet the only composer of his day who can truly be said to come anywhere near comparison with Mozart was Joseph Haydn, master of the string quartet, the symphony and the piano sonata.

Although Mozart achieved success and recognition during his lifetime and was acclaimed as a child prodigy, his true worth was realised only after his death. Like that of many creative artists, his day-to-day life was somewhat precariously balanced, emotionally and financially. Much of his early life

Opposite *A romanticised portrait of Mozart, with a facsimile of his signature.*

Left *Mozart's Walter clavier. This instrument is now in the Mozarteum at Salzburg.*

was spent travelling, composing and performing in the musical courts of Europe. The primary aim of this restless wandering was Leopold Mozart's great desire to find a prestigious musical position for his son. As Wolfgang grew older, he too believed that such an appointment would provide the answer to all his troubles.

Unfortunately, and in spite of his great musical genius, such a stable and exalted position always eluded him. Indeed, the Empress Maria Theresa, although entertained by his musical prowess, recommended that her son should not appoint Mozart to a musical position within his court. In her august opinion, Wolfgang was nothing but a travelling beggar who would degrade the Archduke Ferdinand's service; and this verdict seems to have been shared by almost all the influential aristocracy upon whom Wolfgang depended for preferment.

Mozart composed over six hundred works. These were all catalogued by the nineteenth-century Austrian botanist and mineralogist, Ludwig Ritter von Köchel (whence the Köchel or 'K' numbers used nowadays to identify his works). Köchel's complete catalogue was first published at Leipzig in 1862. Although subsequent musical research has led to a revision of some of the information, particularly some of the composition dates, the Köchel catalogue is regarded as the definitive reference work to this day.

Today Mozart's symphonies, orchestral works and concertos are usually played by smaller groups than was customary until fairly recently. Most recent recordings or concert-hall performances of the symphonies feature chamber orchestras, playing either modern or original eighteenth-century instruments. Such orchestras include the Academy of St Martin-in-the-Fields, the English Chamber Orchestra, the Orchestra of the 18th Century and the Orpheus Chamber Orchestra.

ORCHESTRAL MUSIC

Most of Mozart's orchestral music was written in Salzburg. It consists mainly of serenades and divertimenti written as 'entertainment' music and

Famiglia Asburgo Lorena, by Martin van Mytens – a portrait of members of the imperial house of Habsburg. Empress Maria Theresa, on the right, regarded Mozart as little better than a tramp and blocked his chances of a musical post at the royal court.

The Academy of St Martin-in-the-Fields is typical of the relatively small-scale groups which perform Mozart's orchestral works today.

mostly commissioned for a specific event. One example is the serenade No. 7 in D, the 'Haffner' (K.250). This, as the name implies, was written for the marriage celebrations of the daughter of Sigmund Haffner, a wealthy Salzburg merchant.

Other typical examples are No. 9, in D, the 'Posthorn' (K.320), and – most famous of all – the serenade No. 13 in G, *Eine kleine Nachtmusik* (K.525), which was written in 1787. This piece is scored for a small string band and would originally have had five movements; unfortunately, the second menuetto has been lost. The four movements performed today are an allegro, a romanze, a martial-sounding menuetto with a delightful contrasting trio, and a jolly rondo finale based on a popular Viennese song. In terms of the marriage of form and content the composition is a perfect as any musical work ever written. It is one of the most popular of all his works and has been much copied and adapted.

The commemorative Masonic Funeral music (K.477) was originally written for two members of the Beneficence Lodge to which Mozart belonged.

The other orchestral compositions are mostly sets of contra-dances and minuets written for the Redoutensaal winter balls. Most of these works have been recorded by the Academy of St Martin-in-the Fields, the Dresden State Orchestra, the Prague Chamber Orchestra, the Vienna Mozart Ensemble and the Netherlands Wind Ensemble and other distinguished small groups.

CONCERTOS

Mozart composed concertos for all the leading instruments of his day, except, surprisingly, the cello. Apart from the juvenile piano concertos, the earliest concerto to be included on the fringes of present-day repertoire is the bassoon concerto in B flat (K.191). Mozart gives the 'joker' of the orchestra some hair-raisingly difficult music to play, yet at the same time some beautiful tunes with plenty of verve and spirit.

The five concertos which followed were all for the violin (a sixth concerto exists but is rarely played). Numbers three, four and five – generally considered to be more mature – are the ones most often included in today's concert repertoire. Among the best recordings of these works by the great present-day soloists are those by Itzhak Perlman, Pinchas Zukerman, Anne-Sophie Mutter and Cho-Liang Lin; equally fine versions by an older generation are those by Josef Suk, Wolfgang Schneiderhan, Arthur Grumiaux, Jascha Heifetz and Zino Francescatti.

The flute concertos (K.313 and K.314) were composed next. The latter was a reworking of an earlier oboe concerto which is lost. (The oboe concerto listed in the catalogue is an arrangement of the second flute concerto and has the same K. number.) These were followed by the concerto for flute and harp (K.299).

Between 1781 and 1786 Mozart wrote

Anne-Sophie Mutter, an internationally renowned violinist who has recorded a number of Mozart's violin concertos.

several horn concertos, although only four of these survive intact. Number one has only two movements, so it must be assumed that either the third movement has been lost or that the two existing movements belong to another work. The most famous of these concertos is No. 4 in E flat (K.495). This is scored for two oboes, two horns, strings and the solo horn. The first movement is an allegro moderato which gives the solo horn player the opportunity to display his ability and skill in holding long notes. Mozart appeared to take great delight in composing playful exchanges between the solo instrument and the rest of the orchestra. The second movement, romanze andante, is serene and marvellously soothing in spirit with only an occasional hint of drama. The finale is a typical rondo-à-la-chasse: hunting fanfares abound and the entire movement is imbued with rollicking tunes. This final movement became very popular during the 1960s when the entertainers Michael Flanders and Donald Swann put some witty verses to the main theme. One of the greatest musical exponents of this concerto was the late Dennis Brain. Other great interpreters include Hermann Baumann, Barry Tuckwell and Alan Civil. Baumann has recorded these concertos using a hand-horn – that is, a valveless horn such as Leutgeb, the man for whom the works were originally written, would have played.

The last wind concerto, and indeed the last concerto Mozart wrote in the summer of 1791, not long before his death, was the clarinet concerto in A (K.622). Like all his works for clarinet, it was composed for Mozart's friend and fellow freemason Anton Stadler. Many present-day performers choose to play a basset clarinet, the instrument for which the work was written. Unlike the modern clarinet, this instrument has an extended range which makes it possible to play much lower notes. Exponents using original instruments include Thea King, Anthony Pay and Charles Neidich; those preferring to play modern clarinets include Jack Brymer, Emma Johnson and Karl Leister. The perfect craftsmanship and sublime invention of this masterpiece defies description. Each of the three movements, allegro, adagio and rondo, evokes a singular emotional mood within the listener.

Some of Mozart's early piano concertos were arrangements of other composers' music, such as Raupach, Honauer and J.C. Bach. Mozart wrote twenty-seven piano concertos and these, together with the operas, represent the zenith of his achievement. During 1784 and 1786, Mozart produced one masterpiece after another and it is impossible to state emphatically that one work is better than another. Two concertos, completed in March 1786, are typical examples of his greatness. The concerto No. 23 in A major (K.488) is relatively untroubled and wistful. The opening movement shines with subdued light and grace; the second movement, adagio, is in contrast one of the most poignant pieces he ever wrote. The finale is one of Mozart's happiest and liveliest creations.

The concerto No. 24 in C minor (K.491) is entirely different. It is an extremely sombre, almost tragic work on a grand scale. It is scored for a larger orchestra than any of his other concertos and requires, in addition to the strings, a flute, pairs of oboes, clarinets, bassoons, horns, trumpets, and drums. The second movement provides only a brief respite from the prevailing mood with relaxing reflection; the finale is a set of variations on a march-like theme, rather than the gay rondo Mozart so often favoured. Beethoven is reported to have admired this concerto enormously.

There are many famous interpreters of the piano concertos and modern practice, although not exclusively so, is for a small chamber-sized orchestra led by the soloist from the keyboard. This is the way the concertos would have been performed by Mozart and his contemporaries, and has been widely cultivated today by some of the finest interpreters, including Daniel Barenboim, Mitsuko Uchida, Vladimir Ashkenazy and Murray Perahia. All these artists have recorded the complete concertos for different recording companies, conducting a chamber-sized orchestra from the keyboard. Other notable pianists who have recorded most of Mozart's concertos, although with larger orchestras and separate conductors, are Alfred Brendel, Friedrich Gulda, and Rudolf Serkin. One pianist who plays a forte-piano, an instrument which is very similar to the kind used by Mozart himself, is the American Malcolm Bilson, who has recorded a number of concertos accompanied by the English Baroque Soloists under John Eliot Gardiner.

SYMPHONIES

The compositional span of Mozart's symphonies is almost as great as that of the concertos. The first juvenile works were composed in 1764, when Wolfgang was staying in London, and the last great trilogy, Nos. 39, 40 and 41, were written in 1788. Most of the later symphonies, up to and including No. 36 in C major, the 'Linz' (K.425), are supreme examples of the genre of the late eighteenth century, and one can select movement after movement from these examples alone to show how Mozart's musical genius enriched the symphonic form.

Here we will look briefly at the last four symphonies. No. 37 in the Köchel catalogue is in fact spurious: it was composed by Michael Haydn, with Mozart writing only the introduction to the first movement. No. 38 in D major, the 'Prague' (K.504), is so called because it received its first performance in the Bohemian capital when Wolfgang was staying there to supervise a

production of *The Marriage of Figaro*. The symphony was composed in Vienna; rather strangely, it does not reflect the bubbling gaiety of *Figaro* but looks forward more to Mozart's next operatic commission from Prague, *Don Giovanni*, with its characteristically demonic grandeur. Mozart dispensed with the customary menuetto, perhaps because he thought it would destroy the serious mood or simply because he thought Bohemian audiences preferred three-movement works. His compositional technique underwent a change during this period of his life and the 'Prague' was the first symphonic work to benefit from this more elaborate and serious style. Mozart no longer thought of the symphony as either just a curtain raiser or the grand finale to a concert. Now it had become for him a means of expressing great artistic depths.

Mozart's last three symphonies appeared in quick succession during the summer of 1788. No. 39 in E flat major (K.543) is dated 26 June; No. 40 in G minor (K.550) is dated 25 July; the last, No. 41 in C major, the 'Jupiter' (K.551), is dated 10 August. It is not clear why K.551 was called the 'Jupiter', and there is evidence to suggest that Mozart was not responsible for such a title. The name first appeared in print in the 1820s on a piano arrangement which was made and published in London. It was discovered by music publishers around this time that compositions with a 'nickname' generally sold better than those without. However, there is no doubt that all three symphonies reach a pinnacle of symphonic composition that has rarely been approached and never surpassed.

Daniel Barenboim, the first of the present-day performers to play and record all the Mozart piano concertos, conducting from the keyboard.

A slow introduction opens the first movement of the E flat major symphony – the remaining two symphonies, K.550 and K.551, dispense with this convention – and a jubliant allegro follows. The slow movement, andante con moto, with a march-like principal theme, contrasts with a slightly bizarre theme in the minor key. The menuetto has always been a great favourite and possibly the most famous movement from any of the symphonies ever to be played out of context. The festive brilliance of the opening with its trumpets and drums contrast with the almost hurdy-gurdy effect of the trio with two prominent clarinets; one playing in the upper register, the other in the lower. The finale is Mozart in one of his happiest moods, with prominent woodwind and chuckling bassoon.

Symphony No. 40 in G minor (K.550), without the trumpets and drums of the companion pieces, is the most melancholy of the three with some wonderful melodic writing of great beauty. From the outset we are plunged into a troubled and agitated theme which is followed by one of Mozart's most beautiful melodies. These themes are fully developed before the movement ends in a burst of painful energy. The delicate andante is full of melancholy resignation and the menuetto follows the same disturbing mood; there is little of the carefree feeling usually associated with such a movement – only the trio section has a hint of consolation. The final allegro assai balances the first movement in its energy and with its poignantly beautiful second theme.

The last symphony, No. 41 in C major (K.551), is one of great strength. The opening movement, allegro vivace, has strong dynamic contrasts and a truly Olympian ring to its themes and overall structure. It has a classical perfection in its use of subject matter. The second movement, andante cantabile, has a profound expressive theme reminiscent of a long drawn out song. The menuetto is one of Mozart's stateliest. The final movement represents the peak of Mozart's contrapuntal and symphonic achievements. Every contrapuntal device is employed, even, at one stage, the combination of five themes in a myriad of intricate ways, yet it is not difficult to follow. The expressive final theme blazes forth with trumpet and drums.

Most of the music written during this period is now performed by small groups rather than the larger orchestras such as the Berlin or Vienna Philharmonics. Small orchestras, such as the Academy of St Martin-in-the-Fields or the English Chamber Orchestra using modern instruments, or the Academy of Ancient Music and the Orchestra of the 18th Century playing on period instruments, can provide sprung rhythms and a keener sense of spontaneity than the larger orchestras. Notable Mozart conductors are Herbert von Karajan, Leonard Bernstein, Karl Böhm, Colin Davis, Nikolaus Harnoncourt, Charles Mackerras, Neville Marriner and finally the younger conductors – some specialising in period-instrument groups – such as Daniel Barenboim, Frans Brueggen, Christopher Hogwood, James Conlon and Jeffrey Tate.

CHAMBER MUSIC

In broad terms, chamber music was originally played in a small, often domestic, room as opposed to a large hall. Chamber music is usually played by a small group of players – the maximum is about nine – and the most popular is the string quartet, which comprises two violins, viola and cello.

Mozart wrote twenty-three string quartets, the most famous of which are the six dedicated to Haydn: K.387, K.421, K.428, K.458, K.464 and K.465. These are followed in popularity by the three he wrote for the King of Prussia, Frederick II: K.575, K.589 and K.590.

The six quartets dedicated to Haydn must have been a labour of love; they were not commissioned, nor did Mozart expect to make any money from them. All six quartets rank amongst the most perfect ever written. Their variety of thematic matter and concentration of musical thought make them equally enjoyable to expert and casual listener alike, for the scholarly approach is combined with great emotional appeal. Although Mozart looked upon Haydn's Opus 33 quartets as an object lesson and actually makes direct reference to them in several of the movements, all six quartets are pure Mozart.

Mozart composed only six quintets, yet he displays a compositional mastery in this form equal to that in the Haydn quartets. Some musicologists believe he surpassed even these in the quintets K.515 and K.516 composed in his later years. Mozart loved the rich, dark tonal quality of the viola, so it is no surprise that he added a second viola part to the standard quartet rather than an extra cello, as most other composers have done since.

The quintet in C major (K.515) was completed in April 1787 and its compositional skill is exceeded only by the quintet in G minor (K.516), which he must have been working on at the same time since it was completed four weeks later. Some of Mozart's greatest work is in the minor key and this is a dark, bitter and tormented work with a particularly poignant slow movement.

Mozart wrote a great deal of chamber music for various instrumental combinations – for example, piano trios, piano quartets, and flute quartets – all of which are good examples of his lighter style and certainly no less appealing. Perhaps the greatest chamber work, other than those already mentioned, is the quintet for clarinet and strings in A major (K.581). This serene work leaves the listener in a state of peaceful contentment.

The Amadeus, Gabrieli, Italian, and Melos quartets are supreme exponents of Mozart's chamber music. There are also superb versions by the Alban Berg, Chilingirian and Salomon quartets and others.

VOCAL MUSIC

T he wealth of Mozart's church music was written during his Salzburg years. He also composed several choral pieces for private performances in his masonic lodge. The solo concert arias with

Above
Kammermusik am Kurfurstlichen Hofe zu München *by Johann Nicolaus de Groot, c. 1797: a charming evocation of a domestic musical scene of the period.*

Left Concerto nella Sala dei Filarmonica *by G. Bella shows a more formal concert of the 1790s.*

Aloysia Lange, eldest daughter of Fridolin and Maria Weber. Although Aloysia rejected Wolfgang's romantic advances, she and her husband, the painter Joseph Lange, remained friends with the Mozarts, and Wolfgang married her sister Constanze.

orchestra make up a large number of works for soprano, tenor and bass. At this time it was customary for symphonic movements to be interspersed with short vocal pieces. Most of these works were written for Mozart's friends, such as Josepha Dušek, the Wendling sisters, Anton Raaf, Ludwig Fischer, Aloysia Lange, his sister-in-law, and also for his wife, Constanze. Although Mozart's contribution to church music is not as significant as that of either J.S. Bach or Haydn, it is certainly not negligible and cannot be discounted. The Vespers (K.339) and the mass in C major, the 'Coronation' (K.317), are prime examples with many beautiful movements that ravish the ear and console the heart. The unfinished Mass in C minor (K.427) is consistently great and its incompleteness makes it even more tantalising, although some scholars have added movements from other works. Minor additions are all that it necessary to perform the existing movements, and this is how it is most often played today. The hauntingly beautiful yet very difficult solo soprano aria 'Et incarnatus est' in the credo movement was written expressly for Constanze Mozart.

Apart from Mozart's operas, the Requiem in D minor (K.626) is the vocal work most frequently recorded and performed in the concert hall today. In this work, Mozart banishes most of the brightly coloured woodwind instruments, limiting the remainder to bassoons and basset-horns. The dark coloration of the score is produced by the trombones, trumpets and drums. There are no individual arias for the solo quartet,

instead they blend and contrast with the full choir. Nowhere else in any of Mozart's work do we find such a powerful sense of mourning, coupled with power, glory and piety. Bowing before God, Mozart ends his short life with this final artistic expression of the mysteries of life and death. Haydn believed Mozart deserved immortality for this work alone.

Many of the world's most distinguished choirs have recorded Mozart's church music, including the John Aldis Choir, the Choir of King's College, Cambridge and the Monteverdi Choir. Larger choirs include the Vienna Singverein, the Bavarian Radio Choir and the London Philharmonic Choir. World-famous soloists include Edith Mathis, Kiri Te Kanawa, Helen Donath, Margaret Price, Peter Schreier, Robert Tear, Ryland Davies, John Shirley-Quirk and José van Dam.

THE OPERAS

Mozart was always fascinated by the stage and it is fitting that of his six mature operas, four have remained in the standard repertoire of the world's opera houses. They sum up the operatic experiences of the last two centuries and form an important foundation for all operatic development. In both *The Marriage of Figaro* and *Don Giovanni*, Mozart shows a talent for musical characterisation that few other composers have ever achieved. The first masterwork is *The Abduction from the Seraglio*, which Mozart wrote in 1781–2 for a new German national Singspiel company. He had a very clear idea of the musical and dramatic content he wanted, and the work is a mixture of styles. The portrayal of the manservant is in the style of Italian comic opera; the great dramatic outburst of the heroine in the superb aria, 'Martern aller Arten' is *opera seria*, and the finale has Turkish Janissary music ringing out in a lively march. Osmin, the Pasha's steward, is a pure pantomime character, and one of the most amusing comic bass roles in opera.

In contrast, *The Marriage of Figaro* is the greatest and wittiest comedy in the whole operatic canon, with particularly convincing characters. The pert maidservant, Susanna; her wily bridegroom, Figaro; the lovelorn page, Cherubino; the amorous middle-aged Count and the serious, long-suffering and tragic figure of his Countess. All the frivolous comings and goings are told in a story of intrigue and deception; the situation is finally resolved with life-enhancing reconciliation. The most memorable arias are Cherubino's canzone, 'Voi, che sapete'; Susanna's declaration of love, 'Deh, vieni non tardar' and the Countess's 'Porgi

Don Giovanni in the 1982 production at Glyndebourne. This scene shows the Don (left) ordering his servant, Leporello, to invite the statue of the Commendatore to supper.

Above *In this scene, Don Giovanni meets his retribution and is cast down to Hell.*

amor' and 'Dove sono', expressing in the first her unhappiness at her husband's philanderings and in the second recalling her past happiness. Figaro also has two famous arias, 'Se vuol ballare' and 'Non piu andrai'. The latter, a jaunty martial song, was subsequently used as a basis for all manner of contra-dances and arrangements for different instrumental combinations.

It is astonishing that such a masterpiece should be followed so shortly afterwards by another equally stunning work, *Don Giovanni*. Again the theme is seduction, but this time there is no final reconciliation. Instead there is retribution and vengeance for unrepented past deeds.

This ominous prophecy of doom is immediately set, before the curtain rises, in the overture where the trombone blasts out a theme representing the Don's boldness, with a gloomy, slow introduction conjuring up the supernatural forces of fate. The passions expressed in the opera range from a simple gallant duet, 'Là ci darem la mano', one of Mozart's most famous; the charming serenade with mandolin accompaniment when the Don woos Donna Elvira's maid; the frivolous 'Catalogue' aria in which Leporello lists the Don's conquests, to the horrific and menacing aria sung by the stone statue of the murdered Commendatore who has come to drag the Don down to Hell. In the nineteenth century the opera ended here, omitting the final sextet which comments on the events just past.

Così fan tutte has only recently achieved a wide popularity, for it was once considered to be rather silly or even immoral, in spite of its beautiful melodies. Today it is recognised as a complex investigation of human emotions, finely poised in construction. There is nothing more sensuous than the trio finale in scene two of Act One, when the two ladies bid farewell to their lovers, with

Così fan tutte: *the two suitors, dressed as Albanians, feign death by drinking poison.*

the cynical Don Alfonso adding his comments. The overall style shows a development towards a serene irony.

The Magic Flute, Mozart's last opera, has a simple story about the overthrowing of evil with good. In its day, not everyone responded positively to its mixture of masonic symbolism and moralising with naive comedy. Fortunately, the Viennese love fairy tales and they were entranced by Papageno, the bird catcher with his set of magic bells, and the lovers Tamino and Pamino. In any

case, the delicacy and the greatness of the music could not be disputed and the opera was a huge success, contributing greatly to the fortunes of Emanuel Schikaneder. It is ironic that Mozart was to die just two months later, heavily in debt.

Mozart's operas have attracted the world's greatest singers, conductors and orchestras to the recording studio, and selecting even a shortlist from recordings currently available would be invidious.

Two of the smaller and more intimate

opera houses to stage the Mozart operas regularly are the Festspielhaus in Salzburg and Glyndebourne in Sussex. The latter took its name from the country estate of John Christie and was purpose-built for staging opera performances in ideal surroundings. The first musical festival took place in 1934 with the production of *The Marriage of Figaro* and *Così fan tutte*. The collaboration between the conductor Fritz Busch and the producer Carl Ebert forged new standards for Mozart opera producton

in England and proved influential throughout the world. By the late 1930s the remaining Mozart operas had been added to the repertoire and many of the great singers of the day had performed there. The theatre was closed during the Second World War and reopened in the early 1950s. After the death of Busch, Ebert collaborated with Vittorio Gui.

The most recent conductor to be associated with Glyndebourne is Bernard Haitink, whose recordings have received acclaim.

A scene from Glyndebourne's 1978 production of The Magic Flute, *with sets by David Hockney.*

INDEX

PICTURE ACKNOWLEDGMENTS

The illustration on pages 22–23 is reproduced by gracious permission of Her Majesty the Queen.

Archiv für Kunst und Geschichte 7, 16–17, 23, 27 bottom, 34–35, 36–37, 48–49, 54, 67, 87 top; Austrian National Tourist Office 11 top; Clive Barda 75 left, 83, 84; Bavaria Bildagentur, Jacques Alexandre 43 bottom, Peter Irish 24–25, Messerschmidt 63 top; Bridgeman Art Library 22; British Library 52; Deutsches Theatermuseum 37 left, 37 right; Dominic Photography, Zoë Dominic 51, 63 bottom; E T Archive 59; Mary Evans Picture Library 6, 12, 30 bottom right, 38–39, 46 top, 61, 69, 70, 71, 78 bottom; Gesellschaft der Musikfreunde in Wien 60, 62; Guy Gravett 42, 47, 70–71, 72–73, 78 top, 88–89, 90, 90–91, 92–93; Robert Harding Picture Library 58 top, 66, 79 bottom; Hulton-Deutsch Collection 32–33, 48, 80 top, 80 bottom; Hunterian Art Gallery, University of Glasgow 50; Internationale Stiftung Mozarteum 10, 11 bottom, 18, 19, 34, 40–41, 43 top, 68, 81 bottom, 88; Kunsthistorisches Museum, Vienna 46 bottom, 74; Larousse 56, 81 top; Mansell Collection 14–15, 45, 64; Österreichisches Nationalbibliothek 8–9, 44, 55, 57, 65, 76–77, 77 top; Peters Edition Limited 77 bottom; Polygram Classics 85; Residenz Galerie 31; Royal College of Music 36; Salzburger Museum Carolino Augusteum 9; Scala 26, 27 top, 28–29, 30 bottom left, 75 right, 79 top, 82, 87 bottom; ZEFA 13, 58 bottom; ZEFA, Halin 30 top, Studio Benser 20–21, Stuller 53.

Front cover, centre left ZEFA/L. Sitensky